THE SIRTFOOD DIET
THE COMPLETE COOKBOOK!

Activate Your Skinny Gene, Lose Weight, Burn Fat & Get Lean (Includes A Step-By-Step 21 Days Meal Plan With Recipes!)

Andrew Werner

TABLE OF CONTENTS

CHAPTER ONE
INTRODUCTION

Losing weight and developing a perfect body are some of the most common aspirations among individuals from different cultures, backgrounds, social classes, and genders around the world. Virtually everyone wants to lose weight and look trim and attractive. Some people have deeper and more far-reaching reasons for wanting to lose weight, however. Amanda, 50, is an experienced interior decorator and events planner who runs a successful business in Chicago. Amanda's life is almost perfect – she has a brilliant engineer husband who also earns a great pay, three beautiful kids, one done with college and the other two in great programs at their respective colleges. She and her dear husband, John, live in their beautiful home in Illinois, the mortgage fully paid for. They even manage to go on exotic vacations to Europe and the Caribbean once or twice a year.

The problem, however, is that Amanda has an unhealthy addiction to sugary foods, much like a lot of Americans and individuals living in first-world countries. She developed her addiction to sugary foods in her college days and the early days of her career as a public accountant. She was constantly stressed because of the pressures of the job, and she constantly snacked on pastries, candy, and chocolate bars to stave off boredom and help her feel full at work. Kicking the habit became almost impossible. At first, it didn't seem much like a problem, and she didn't mind the few extra pounds she seemed to gain every now and then.

However, a few days to her fortieth birthday ten years ago, Amanda wanted to take a picture for her birthday, and it hit her how much weight she had put on. She felt guilty and a tad unattractive when she saw the pictures, and they served as a liberating sign for her to do something about her weight. She discussed with her doctor, who referred her to a nutritionist, who advised her to begin a dieting regimen that would help her cut back on her calorie consumption. The nutritionist wasn't, however, considering one fundamental problem – Amanda's debilitating addiction to sugary foods. Amanda barely survived three weeks on her new diet when she began to sneak in chocolate cake in her bag to work. Soon, she slipped off the wagon entirely and went back to her old, unhealthy eating habits.

All through her forties, Amanda tried out several weight loss programs and 'magic' products. Most predictably turned out to be a waste of time, effort, and money. It wasn't that these regimens and products were entirely useless, the problem was that they forced her to suddenly and drastically cut down her calorie consumption, and that was just an impossible task for Amanda to accomplish. Now, a few months after her fiftieth birthday, her doctor has told her that she suffers a great risk of developing high blood pressure because all the fat in her body is beginning to take a toll on her heart and the pressure with which it needs to pump blood around her body.

A lot of people in developed and developing countries are like Amanda. At one point or the other in our lives, we consciously or subconsciously pick up the habit of over-eating sweet foods rich in processed sugars and low in essential nutrients. This habit fast becomes an addiction, but almost everyone around us seems to be doing it, so we don't really care. Eventually, we get a wake-up call, while some of us do not. Either way, we tend to end up overweight, or with some health challenges as a result of our terrible over-consumption of unhealthy junk food.

The ambition of this book is to help you build a sustainable system that would enable you to lose weight without falling off the wagon and feeling frustrated. At least half of overweight Americans have tried some type of weight-loss regimen at one point or the other in their lives. More often than not, these people are not able to sustain these strict diets because of their addiction to binge-eating and the feeling of being full. The goal of this entire system, therefore, is to help you, in a step-by-step and day-by-day manner, to formulate a specialized diet that allows you to eat enough food to power through your daily activities while helping you to gradually reduce body fat while maintaining or consolidating on your body's muscle mass. This is basically an eating plan that allows you to lose weight without feeling starved or terribly lethargic effectively. The special, systematic diet is called the sirtfood diet.

Before moving on to describe how the sirtfood diet works, I believe it would be critically important at this point to review the psychology behind building a system that works instead of rushing blindly to achieve giant, lofty, and most times, unattainable goals. In dieting, and in life in general, we all tend to make lots of huge important goals. A student in a college may say to himself: "This semester, I want to have at least a 3.5 GPA out of the maximum possible 4.0. A car salesman may say to himself: "This month, I want to sell enough cars to make at least ten thousand dollars in commissions." A person trying to lose weight may say: "This week, I'll exercise hard, rest well and watch every single thing I eat so that by the end of the week, I would have lost at least 10 pounds." These are all relatively reasonable goals that the average individual can attain if they put in enough hard work. The complication, however, is usually that most people are so fixated on the goal that they want to achieve; they fantasize about how amazing it would be to have that dream GPA, dream monthly income or dream figure, that they do not focus enough on how the day-to-day execution of their plans to achieve their goals would go. Eventually, because of their fixation on a goal and not a system to help them achieve that goal, they end up, more often than not, failing to meet their desired targets.

Don't get me wrong; having the goal to lose ten pounds a week is a fantastic one, and if you watch your diet and exercise quite vigorously while sleeping well, you can actually crush that goal. However, the only way you are going to crush that goal is if you are able to draft out a plan that you can follow on a day-to-day basis to help you achieve that goal. The goal is most definitely not going to achieve itself. However, when you have a system in place to help you achieve your long-term academic, income, or weight goals, then your job becomes significantly easier. Instead of being fixated on the final goal, you become addicted to meeting your small, daily targets. And we all know that crushing small daily goals is easier than blindly trying to chase a big one without a plan.

The sirtfood diet is a system, not a goal. The sirtfood diet is meant to help you develop a sustainable eating routine that doesn't necessitate you to go hungry. With the sirtfood diet, you do not have to cope with the constant fatigue, lethargy, lack of motivation, and eventual relapse into unhealthy eating that comes with most diets. This is simply because of one fact – the diet has been well-researched and properly tested, and has been designed to help you crush your weight-loss goals comfortably, one day at a time.

When you get engaged in the sirtfood diet, you will actually become so obsessed with making sure that you are following the system (getting healthy can be addictive too!) that you would just gaze at the mirror one day and realize that paying so much attention to following your system has helped you to attain your goals without you being so fixated on them.

You may wonder if the sirtfood diet is only effective for a specific set of individuals. The sirtfood diet has been proven to be effective in promoting weight loss, increased energy levels, and improved mental health among a wide variety of people. Generally, every single aspect of the population can benefit from the sirtfood diet model. Some of the most important beneficiaries of the diet, however, include:

- Overweight people: To gauge obesity, weight is generally calculated in terms of an individual's body mass index, which is obtained by dividing an individual's body mass by their weight in squared meters. Generally, adults with a BMI above $25kg/m^2$ are considered overweight, while individuals with a BMI above $30kg/m^2$ are considered obese and need to get to work right away on their weight lest they suffer dangerous health consequences. Generally, children and adolescents with BMIs exceeding $20kg/m^2$ need to seek adequate medical attention and advice on how to curb their weight gain and prevent far-reaching complications.

- Since the sirtfood diet is designed to help people lose weight without putting too much pressure on them psychologically, physically, and financially, it is a perfect weight-loss option for slightly overweight and morbidly obese individuals. The diet is simple, contains foods that are delicious and enjoyable, and does not require the individual to go unnecessarily hungry. The availability of energy for the dieting individual and the feeling of satiation after the meals in the diet will help ensure that the overweight individual does not fall into his old, unhealthy eating habits. The special collection of foods that make up the sirtfood diet and their active ingredients will then help to set off a series of reactions within the body, which will instigate rapid and sustainable weight loss. The sirtfood diet can, therefore, be a reliable means to help mitigate life-threatening obesity and slightly excess weight without putting the individual under undue pressure.

- Old people: Older members of the population are quite predisposed to gaining unhealthy weight that they may find it quite difficult to shed. Old people generally tend to engage in less strenuous or physically-demanding activities. Hence, most of the fats they consume end up stored within their bodies. The sirtfood diet, however, can be an enjoyable and sustainable technique to help older people lose weight without putting them through the undue and unrealistic rigors of extreme exercise or crippling diets. With the sirtfood diet, senior citizens can eat a selected collection of healthy foods at regular intervals to help them stay satiated and energized while losing weight and building necessary muscle mass.

- Thin or Anorexic People: It's understandable that you might not have thought extremely thin people would be a target of a weight-loss diet, but the sirtfood diet ins truly unique, and it does have something to offer everyone. The specialized chemicals that are released from the carefully selected foods that make up the sirtfood diet do not only help to burn unwanted fat; they also help to build muscle mass within the body. How on earth can the same diet plan help to reduce fat while at the same time helping to boost muscle mass? Just hold your breath and keep reading. You'll find out exactly how the sirtfood diet carries out these two seemingly contradictory functions in perfect harmony in the next couple of pages.

- Fitness Enthusiasts: If you are neither overweight nor extremely thin, but you would like to get in shape and look fitter, trimmer, and more attractive, then the sirtfood diet can work wonderfully well with light exercise regimens to help give you the body of your dreams. The sirtfood diet is reputed for its ability to help decimate fat stores in the body while helping to rapidly burgeon the body's muscle mass. Therefore, if you've been on the hunt, searching for the perfect set of foods that would help complement your efforts in the gym, then you have just found the exact solution that you have been looking for. Experts even say that with the sirtfood diet, you do not necessarily have to undergo hours of rigorous exercise at the gym to gain the body of your dreams. With a carefully reviewed home workout schedule and running in the morning about thrice a week, you should be able to get your dream body carved out while, of course, integrating the sirtfood diet into your food timetable.

- Young people: This is another section of the population that can benefit immensely from the merits that the sirtfood diet has to offer. Young people are usually highly-active individuals who lead pretty high-powered lifestyles – college, a demanding job, partying with friends, playing games and sports...the list of the things that take up the time and energies of young people is almost endless. Because of their demanding lifestyle, young people need as much energy as they can. Piling up fat in the body will naturally make an individual feel fatigued faster. The sirtfood diet can help young people, irrespective of their body size to build muscle mass, increase their energy levels on a daily basis and help them increase their mental alertness to perform superbly well at intellectual tasks.

- Career professionals: If you work in a demanding segment of the economy – for instance in a hospital, a financial services firm, or you run your own small business, then you will agree with me that you can never have too much energy or alertness. Most individuals are active and alert at work in the first half of the day. Later in the day, usually from mid-afternoon, most professionals experience a drop in their energy levels, leading to a significant dip in performance and results. To help you stay optimally motivated and energized throughout your day, the sirtfood diet contains specialized natural chemical substances that will help your body to extract the maximum amount of energy possible from the natural foods you eat. The foods in the sirtfood diet will also help you to build muscle mass and lose weight as a busy professional, thereby helping you to be more confident at work.

Who you're absolutely doesn't matter, what you do, or what your performance goals are. As long as you want to have more energy to help you through your daily life, build muscle mass to help you feel stronger while burning excess, healthy fats, and you want to generally feel healthier and more mentally alert, then the sirtfood diet can be an extremely important tool to help you achieve your body goals and help you begin a journey to high performance and superb health.

So, as you plan to begin this journey to this new revolutionary dietary lifestyle, I'm here to make you a promise. That promise is that within a week of sticking religiously to this sirtfood diet, you will lose at least 5 to 7 pounds. Within that first week, you will feel your energy levels rise noticeably, you will feel your moods improve, and you will experience a new, noticeable feeling of increased general wellbeing.

If you stick to this program till the end of the first month and combine it with a healthy lifestyle, such as regular moderate exercise and a healthy lifestyle, you will feel your need to consume the unhealthy foods you were previously addicted to decrease. Your weight loss will continue; you'll drop another few pounds of fat and increase your body's muscle mass. You will experience a noticeable increase in clarity and alertness at work and at home. Your moods will improve, and so will your sleep. You will actually feel like you've just secured a new lease on life.

The sirtfoods immense impact on our lives is because of the far-reaching effects that the foods that we put in our bodies have on our general wellbeing. Most people do not understand just how critical then the food we consume is to our lies. When you eat too much sugar, saturated fats, and unhealthy food, you pile your body with unnecessary stores of fats. These fat stores are not adequately metabolized in time because you keep eating these unhealthy foods at regular intervals. The fat stores make you feel lethargic and slow, they make it difficult to exercise and work efficiently, and they may even have long-term adverse effects on your health – especially the efficiency of your cardiovascular system. When you take up a new healthy diet, you give your body newer, cleaner fuel to run on. You can think of sirtfoods as clean energy for your body's ecosystem. The former foods you were consuming were causing pollution and simply clogging up your body's landscape with unhealthy fats and harmful unwanted compounds. Once you choose to run your body on clean energy, you effectively cut off the source of the pollution. Gradually, your body will begin to let go of the toxic deposits, and your entire body system will feel rejuvenated.

The sirtfood diet, unlike most of the other specialized diets out there, is actually very practical and affordable. I've seen diet plans that force you to eke out thousands of dollars for a month's worth of food. What's more, these foods are complicated to prepare, and they aren't things you can wake up in the morning, put together, and eat before going to work. Practicality and affordability are huge deciding factors in the eventual success or failure of any particular diet. All the foods that make up the sirtfood diet can be prepared from the regular food products you can purchase from your regional grocery. The recipes are also simple and straightforward, and in a matter of minutes, your food is done, you can eat and get yourself off to work or school.

The practicability of the sirtfood diet is not only in its affordability and ease of preparation; however, it's also in its ability to keep you satiated and motivated to work. The basis of most diets is to get you to consume as little food as possible. This technique helps to burn fat in the short term, but it also withers the body's muscle mass and makes the individual feel lazy, less energized, and generally fatigued. The sirtfood diet capitalizes on you eating enough food to work, so it helps you to stay focused and helps to effectively ward off all your unhealthy cravings.

Why exactly am I making these promises about the Sirtfood diet to you? I can confidently make huge statements about the sirtfood diet because it is a dieting regimen that has been tested to be effective and as well trusted to deliver results over the years. The diet itself has been clearly designed to only include a select variety of foods that possess extremely special properties that lead to weight loss, muscle gain, and mental clarity. In thousands of people, the sirtfood diet has helped to recondition body metabolism and improve the overall quality of life.

How quickly will the results of the sirtfood diet show? According to average results from a variety of studies, as mentioned earlier, you should be able to knock about 5 to 7 pounds of pure fat off your body within the first week of taking up the sirtfood diet. Within a month, you could be looking at up to 20 pounds of fat lost, and a respectable gain in muscle.

Since the sirtfood diet helps to burn fat and maintain or gain muscle mass, your weighing scale may not be such a good tool to help judge your progress. Instead, it is advisable for you to watch out for signs of fat loss around your abdomen and waistline. If you find that you have to move your belt buckle up a notch, or your skirts fit better around your waist, then you may have your signs that the sirtfood diet is indeed helping you to burn fat. You will also find your ability to concentrate soar within the first few weeks of starting this diet. You will feel your home workouts translating to more muscle gain since you are now eating to synergize with your exercise, not to antagonize it. Within a month of the sirtfood diet, your sugar cravings will drop extensively, and the gradual drop in fat will have positive effects on your blood pressure.

In a pilot study conducted among 40 participants at a fitness clinic in London, England, the powers of the sirtfood diet were revealed, and they were magnificent. It is one thing to predict the powers of these foods, and it is another thing to experience their effects within a short time frame. During the course of the pilot study, the 20 main foods that make up the sirtfood diet were carefully combined to create the sirtfood diet for the participants. The study was carried out under strictly controlled conditions; the fitness clinic had its own in-house restaurant, so there was no need for the food to be sourced externally. A lot of the participants were already previously healthy people, so the diet had to be super-effective for it to have produced such remarkable results on them.

For seven days, the progress of the individuals who undertook the program was closely monitored. Their weight, changes in body composition, fat and muscle levels, and their blood sugar levels were all carefully tracked. For the first three-to-four days of the week that the study was carried out, the individuals all consumed a maximum of 1000 calories per day. This calorie restriction is necessary for the first phase of the Sirtfood diet. However, since this strict restriction only applies to the first three days of the first phase, it was quite easy for the participants to adhere to it. In the last four days of the study, the participants were allowed to consume up to 1500 calories per day. After the initial stages, you can up your calorie consumption as long as you are not consuming prohibited foods.

Of the 40 individuals who began the sirtfood diet, 39 were able to successfully complete it, representing a 97.5% adherence rate. Basically, there is a 97.5% chance that you would be able to at least make it through the first phase of this incredible diet. And if you make it through the first week, which is the most difficult part, transitioning to the easier second phase where you get to eat even more would not be such a herculean task. When the fat and muscle statistics of the 39 people who completed the study were checked, it was discovered that the group lost an average of 7 pounds of fat in the first week. Most of them maintained their muscle mass, or even gained a bit more. This muscle gains and feeling of satiety is what makes the sirtfood regimen so outstanding and unique. On average, each participant was found to have lost reasonable fat around the waistline and abdominal region. The average participant didn't complain of hunger since the diet has been designed to keep you satiated and energized while burning fat. The average participant reported greater vigor and drive to work and attack their daily goals. What's more, within a week, most of the participants were already looking quite trimmer than they did at the start of the regimen.

So, what particularly do you hope to gain from this sirtfood diet? In the nearest future, if you stick to the sirtfood diet regimen as religiously as possible, this diet will help you achieve a couple of interesting life goals. Imagine a future where you do not ever have to worry about your unhealthy sugar cravings again because you are constantly energized and satiated by your consumption of healthy food. Imagine a future where you are just randomly walking in the park, and someone who knew you from a year ago walks up to you and can't believe their eyes because all your fat has been transformed into solid, healthy muscle. Imagine a future where every time you visit the doctor, you get a clean bill of health instead of a warning that your heart might buckle under the strain of your fat soon. Imagine a future where you walk into work filled with a power meal, and you're ready to crush all your goals for the day without breaking a sweat. Imagine a future filled with fewer hospital visits, more incredible times spent with family, and better achievements at work. Imagine a future with a happier, healthier, and more accomplished you. This future is what the sirtfood diet combined with a healthy lifestyle, can give you.

Now that you have a firm perception of what this book is about and the kind of life you are about to be introduced to, it is time to step things up a notch and take you into the nitty-gritty of what exactly the sirtfood diet is.

CHAPTER TWO
WHAT IS THE SIRTFOOD DIET?

The term 'sirtfood' refers to a natural or slightly processed food item that contains a set of special chemicals known as polyphenols. The polyphenols in the sirtfoods have the ability to lead to the activation of a set of genes in the body known as 'sirtuins.' The sirtuins are also known as skinny genes, and when they are activated, they are able to trigger weight loss in a person. That's basically how sirtfoods work, in a nutshell. Now, let's go a little bit into the technical details.

Most dietary plans work on the basis of reducing the number of calories that a person consumes. This technique works in theory, but it is almost always doomed to fail in the real world. Human beings are not machines or computers, and making huge, sudden changes to something as fundamental to our lives as our diet is almost always impossible. Most diets require you to rapidly cut down on the number of calories you consume per day. A lot of fitness fads are usually seen calculating the number of calories of food they think they might have ingested within a day. When followed properly, calorie-restricting diets have the ability to make people lose weight, but that's about where the benefits stop. A calorie-restricted diet tightly regulates the amount of food that you pass into your body system. This means that your body is forced to burn its fat deposits to gain energy, but once those deposits are gone, then your muscle mass begins to slowly wither. Instead of looking trim and fit during these caloric-restricting diets, a lot of people end up looking pitifully thin as their muscle mass continues to wither away. The drastic drop in calories consumed also has other immediate effects – the person constantly feels hungry, irritated, and fatigued. The phrase: "A hungry man is an angry man" comes into play quite well here.

When on a calorie-restricting diet, the entire body is placed on a limited supply of the fuel it needs to run, and yet the individual is expected to function efficiently. The huger and irritation that the person feels would soon begin to affect all the other aspects of his life. He may find it difficult to concentrate at work due to his new strict diet that forces him to keep close tabs on the number of calories of food he eats per day. Performing even the easiest physical tasks may become difficult, and the body can slowly begin to break down. It is not exceptional to hear of people on these strict diets simply fainting when under immense stress and pressure since they are trying to overwork a body system that is basically running on fumes.

Calorie-restricting diets soon stretch their tentacles into the immune system and may predispose the individual to diseases. The foods that we eat contain essential nutrients and vitamins that help us to keep our bodies in optimal shape. Carbohydrates provide energy, and so do fats. Fat deposits can help to provide warmth. Proteins help to build muscle mass and ensure the proper replication of cells within the body. Vitamins and mineral salts serve essential functions in preventing diseases and keeping important body organs such as the kidneys and liver in perfect shape. When people suddenly restrict their calories without giving their body system a chance to gradually adjust the immune system can take a severe hit. The body isn't being supplied with the natural biochemical it needs to function optimally anymore, so it becomes vulnerable to disease.

Finally, more often than not, the strain of a calorie-restricting diet becomes too much for the individual to bear. If the person used to be addicted to sugary and junk foods before, the strain is even greater. Half the time, they are hungry, and the only thing they can think about is dashing to the snack shop down the street and grabbing some doughnuts and a soda. Eventually, the body is just not able to take the strain anymore, and the person goes right back to their former unhealthy diet. Like a hailstorm, the fats come rushing back, and in a matter of weeks, the person is back right where they started – fat, unhealthy, and unhappy. It's a brutally vicious cycle – one that only a truly sustainable diet like the sirtfood diet can break.

The sirtfood routine, as has been mentioned earlier, contains a variety of select foods, mostly green leafy vegetables, whole grains, cocoa, coffee, and even dark chocolate and red wine! Unlike most of these tough unrealistic diets out there, the sirtfood routine is out to prove to the world that people can actually become healthier and fitter while still eating interesting and tasty foods. Of course, if you are going to be successful with the sirtfood diet, you are going to have to cut back on a couple of harmful foods, but you would be too busy enjoying the delicious new options on your new menu that you wouldn't care about the former foods that only used to stuff you up with pounds upon pounds of fat anyway.

All foods certified as sirtfood have all been extensively analyzed to understand their compositions and their effects on the body. One thing that has been found in all sirtfoods is that they contain a couple of compounds known collectively as polyphenols. The first sirtfood was analyzed in the 20th century, and it was the skin of red grapes used in making red wine. During the analysis of these skins, it was found out that these skins contained a polyphenol known as resveratrol. It had been noted earlier that unlike people who drink heavily alcoholic drinks, people who drink red wine do not tend to get unhealthy or overweight. Instead, red wine drinkers seemed to be svelte, fit, and naturally energetic.

Scientists dug further into how resveratrol, one of the most active compounds in red wine, could be affecting the burning of fat deposits and the maintenance of a trim body figure with a moderate muscle mass within the body. Their findings were nothing short of revolutionary. In their studies, these scientists found out that there are a set of genes located in our bodies known as sirtuins. There are seven sirtuins in total, and they all work together in a system. Each sirtuin is named in a simple manner. The first sirtuin gene is named SIRT 1, the second; SIRT 2, and the numbering goes on like that, reaching SIRT 7. SIRT 1 and SIRT 3 have been found out to be the most active genes in the family of the sirtuins.

Sirtuins are a group of genes known as inducible genes. There are several other genes located throughout the body that work using a similar mechanism as the sirtuins. They stay, relatively hidden and unnoticed within the body. However, when a condition arises that necessitates them to swing into action, inducible genes become activated. They do not just become activated magically, however. They are activated in response to the situation that necessities their attention. You can think of them like firemen. Firemen do not just drive their trucks and come to your house. Your house has to be on fire, and you need to call their attention to the fire. The signal that is sent to the firemen in the form of your phone call or that of your neighbors then forces the firemen to spring into action to come and put out the fire – the incident that led to them getting invited in the first place. This analogy works very well with the sirtuins. The sirtuins remain dormant over the lives of most people because they are not activated. However, when they are activated with the right signals, sirtuins perform an extremely wonderful function – they put the entire body in survival mode and aim to save the body, just like firemen saving a house. To help the body have as much energy as possible to survive the 'perilous' times that the sirtuins believe the body is in, these genes burn up stores of fat within the body to provide energy. The deploy mechanisms to repair and rejuvenate damaged cells, and they boost the abilities of the body's immune system, making the body even more resistant to disease.

Now, there remains one major question. Why on earth would sirtuins think the body is in danger and get activated? The answer is sirtfoods. Sirtfoods contain polyphenols, and the way the regimen is designed, in your first few days of consuming sirtfoods, your calorie intake is reasonably restricted. In the first three days, your calorie intake is restricted to 1000 calories, and in the last four days of the first phase, your calorie intake is restricted to 1500 calories. The combination of the influx of polyphenols into the body and the drastic reduction in the consumption of calories in the first week leads to the activation of a stress pathway within the body. This stress pathway ends in the activation of the previously dormant sirtuins genes. This is where the magic happens. Once the sirtuin genes are activated, the genes serve as directors – much like the corporate executives of a Fortune

500 company. They direct the body mechanisms under their command to burn up the stores of fat within the body to ensure that the body is supplied with the energy it needs to keep running in the wake of the restriction of calories entering the body. The sirtuins also send forth a series of signals which enable another set of mechanisms to clean out toxic materials from cells and rejuvenate ailing body cells. The sirtuins deploy another set of mechanisms to boost the body's immune system to protect the body against any possible attack.

The sirtuins carry out their job efficiently, and as long as the polyphenols continue to stream continuously into the body, the sirtuin genes remain activated and continue their essential duties of directing the burning up of fats and building body cells —which leads to muscular gain. As the presence of the sirtuins 9n your body becomes stable, the sirtuins diet allows you to gradually ease up on the restriction of calories and actually eat more food. The sirtuins have already been activated and established. Once the body is no longer under the stress of calorie restriction, and the polyphenols keep flowing in, the sirtuins bloom and become stable, steadily directing all essential functions leading to weight loss, abundant energy, muscle gain, and supercharged immunity.

For the first few days of the sirtfood diet, it is possible for you to experience a couple of downsides. These downsides are especially more noticeable in the first three days of the first phase (i.e., first week) of the diet. Because of the drastic reduction of your calorie consumption to a thousand calories per day, you may experience hunger, slight irritability, and slight fatigue. These effects are only noticeably pronounced if you used to be a heavy eater. However, keep in mind that the first three days represent the small sacrifice that you have to make for the greater good that is to come. As soon as you hit day 4, you are free to increase your daily consumption to 1500 calories, and after the first week, you can comfortably go back to eating three healthy meals per day while still keeping your sirtuins genes at work; transforming your body.

What are the foods that make up the sirtfood diet? Twenty primary foods have been discovered to contain the concentration of polyphenols needed to activate the sirtuin genes. When these sirtfoods are combined in harmony over a period of time – their effects help to produce wonderful results. There are other permitted foods that also contain reasonable amounts of polyphenols, and those would be discussed in later chapters. Cocoa, extra virgin olive oil, red onions, garlic, parsley, chilies, kale, strawberries, walnuts, capers, tofu, and green tea, are some of the foods that are recommended as part of the sirtfood diet. A full list of the 20 foods that make up the sirtfood diet and their active polyphenols would be given later in this book. These foods have incredible fat burning effects and still contribute an ample number of essential ingredients to improve the functioning of the body system. When consumed together, these foods have a collectively spectacular effect.

You may wonder, are there any people who have benefitted from the sirtfood diet? Yes, definitely, there are. Apart from the 40-man study conducted in London, several people have tried out the sirtfood diet, and have confirmed it to be a truly revolutionary technique to lose weight while retaining muscle and staying energized.

Adele, the popular English singer, and multiple Grammy award winner, is one of the few celebrities who swear by the power of the sirtfood diet. In the early months of 2020, Adele's social media posts have shown her to have cut down on her body fat, making her look trimmer and visibly more energetic. When questioned about her new look and the renewed palpable zest she attacked life with, Adele had a simple answer: The sirtfood diet.

Another individual who has benefitted immensely from the benefits of the sirtfood diet is a TV presenter named Laura. Laura is 29-years old and is an attractive TV sports reporter with a blossoming career. Whether we care to admit it or not, the success of the career of a person who faces millions of people daily depends quite heavily on their looks. Laura has always been a hardworking and talented TV presenter, but her stunning looks sure did add to her appeal as a TV personality. However, as Laura hit her late 20s, she noticed a strange and rather unwelcome development – she was beginning to put on some considerable weight. At first, she didn't think much about it, as it only made her curvier and rounded, but as she grew older, the weight only piled up more till she realized that she needed to do something. Laura confesses that she has battled a debilitating sugar addiction since her late teens. Like a lot of Americans, Laura had subconsciously integrated the habit of eating a lot of sugary snacks into her daily routine. Her work in the media industry was pretty demanding, so in between TV programs and getting ready to host a show, she found herself eating a lot of sugary snacks to stay satiated and feel energized.

However, her addiction was finally coming back to haunt her. She couldn't afford to lose her looks at this point in her career – she needed to look prim and fit; she didn't just want to. Laura confessed to being so hooked on sugar that she carried a bottle of syrup in her handbag to apply to coffee and pastries that she felt were just not sweet enough for her liking. Did she know that excessive sugar consumption was bad for her health? Yes. Did she care? Yes, she did. Could she willingly quit her excessive sugar consumption? Sadly, the answer to that was No.

In an attempt to proffer an effective solution to her weight problems, Laura ventured into the world of dieting. At first, she tried some of the numerous calorie-restricting diet options recommended by most weight-loss experts online and offline. She managed to stay dedicated to some of these diets for a while; she just couldn't bear the strict nature of some. Eventually, every single time, she found herself going back to her beloved junk food. Laura felt helpless – and then discovered the sirtfood regimen.

Within two weeks of eating sirtfoods, Laura's cravings had dipped. This was the first breakthrough for her. To prevent her from gaining even more weight, she always felt guilty of consuming too many calories, but just couldn't help the junk snacks. However, with the sirtfood diet, she was free to eat enough food to get her satiated –which wasn't a lot. This translated to her getting less hungry and being able to carry out her tasks more efficiently. With the excess sugar out of her system, her brain fog slowly cleared, and she found herself getting more focused and motivated at work. Laura's fat slowly melted away. She lost 10 pounds in the first three weeks, and her steady fat loss continued as she regained her dream trim, fit figure which looked superb in anything she wore – whether it was a conservative shirt tucked into a skirt or a tasteful dinner gown. In the long-term, Laura confessed to feeling truly more alive, and she had even managed to cut down on the costs she incurred on purchasing her sugary treats – she hadn't only saved her career, she had saved her health and her wallet too. Call that a three-pronged victory.

The sirtfood diet is not all about external looks; however, as Robert's story teaches us. Rob was a regular middle-aged guy in his forties who suffered from a serious case of depression. Robert was constantly on antidepressants and sedatives, and he relied heavily on these drugs to function as normally as possible. A lot of times, Robert felt like giving up. At work and at home, he tended to move mechanically as if in a daze, and his mind was constantly clouded with worry. Despite the powerful sedatives that he used, on many nights, Robert would lie awake in bed, closing his eyes for long stretches of time but unable to find sleep because of the thoughts raging in his mind. Robert was a truly intelligent man, but his own mind was holding him down and preventing him from achieving his full potential.

Robert's perpetual inactivity caused him to begin to gain weight over time. It wasn't like he was particularly concerned about that anyway; he had bigger problems going on in his head. However, he managed to discover the sirtfood diet, and in two weeks, Robert had managed to lose his first ten pounds of fat. That was not the most revolutionary change for him, however. For the first time in years, Robert managed to go through a week without having to battle his usual bouts of insomnia. Like magic, his self-esteem and personal happiness returned. His colleagues claimed they'd never seen Robert so happy to come to work. He seemed to have a glint in his eyes and a smile for everyone. Consequent to Robert's new diet, he found out that his general mood and his sleep pattern improved, he lost fat, especially around his abdominal region, and he felt himself look actually, fitter.

Melanie was a middle-aged woman with lupus. She was constantly down from the repeated pains and aches that the disease caused. Her condition caused her to be quite inactive, causing her to put on quite a lot of unhealthy fat. Two weeks after she got on the sirtfood diet, her moods drastically improved, and her pains began to slowly dissipate. The polyphenols in the sirtfoods she was consuming activated her body's stress pathways causing her body to use up the fat and spurring the rejuvenation of her body's cells, including her diseased skin cells. Within two weeks, Melanie had managed to drop 11.5 pounds of fat, and her pains and aches were relieved greatly.

Now that we have examined some cases of individuals who have tried the sirtfood diet and experienced spectacular results, how about we back up these stories by looking at entire cultures and civilizations whose meals consist mainly of polyphenol-containing foods?

When the country of Japan is mentioned, different people think of different things. Some people instantly imagine the clean streets and the lively, colorful culture. Some people are reminded of the discipline embedded in the culture of the Japanese. Some people are reminded of their technological prowess. Some people are reminded of their local cuisine, which consists of a lot of leafy vegetables. Whichever imagination you get first when you think of Japan, the truth is that the Japs are quite formidable people. There is, however, a subset of the Japanese who live in a province known as Okinawa. The people in this region have a local cuisine that consists almost exclusively of sirtfoods. The people in this region are rarely obese, have a relatively high life expectancy compared to most other regions of the world, and they are generally referred to as 'happy and lively.' The region is basically pulsating with life and excitement because the people don't stuff themselves with unhealthy junk food. Instead, they have grown up reaping the benefits of a diet that helps them to maintain amazing moods and incredible, fit bodies.

The Native Mediterranean region is another part of the world reputed for its healthy population and its happy people. The Native Mediterranean people have one of the lowest obesity and heart disease rates in the world. Their diets consist majorly of important sirtfoods such as extra virgin olive oil, wild leafy greens, nuts, berries, dates, and red wine. It is exceptionally rare to find a person with a weight problem in this region, and these individuals live in perfect harmony with nature. It is not uncommon to find people living in cottages with lush gardens, and instead of counting calories and using manufactured drugs, these people simply choose to embrace nature by sticking to a healthy and nutritious diet.

So, there you have it. The sirtfood diet has been explained. Some of the people who have successfully used the diet to improve their physical and mental health have been highlighted. Entire cultures that have depended on sirtfood for generations upon generations for superb health and unrivaled happiness have been mentioned. Now, you may wonder: Exactly how effective is the sirtfood diet?

One of the strongest arguments in favor of sirtfoods is easy accessibility. With a trip to your regional grocery store, you can easily purchase the majority of the groceries that you need to prepare the foods in the sirtfood diet. The diet is affordable and easily accessible. A lot of less effective diets require you to purchase expensive supplements and scarce commodities, which make the practicability of these diets even less likely.

Because the aim of the diet is to fill you up with enough healthy foods instead of stripping you of tour necessary daily food supply, it is easier for you to stick to the diet in the long term, making it a very effective weight-loss option. Combined with light exercise and great lifestyle habits, the sirtfood doesn't only help to reform your physical outlook but also has great positive effects on your mental health.

Some of the trackable and significant effects of the sirtfood diet include:

- Fat loss

- Less risk of heart disease

- Fit, trim looks

- Increased energy and motivation

- Less hunger

- Improved physical strength.

Why are the foods allowed to be consumed in the sirtfood diet so beneficial? The answer is simple and straightforward, as we have examined earlier. Sirtfoods have all been carefully selected because they contain a specialized set of natural chemicals known as polyphenols. The polyphenols and the initial restriction of calories work together to activate the body's natural stress pathways, leading to the activation of the sirtuin genes. The sirtuin genes then direct the synthesis and deployment of natural body mechanisms that help to break down fat deposits to supply energy, rejuvenate and revitalize body cells and strengthen the body's natural immune system. The key factors, once again that make the sirtfood diet so beneficial are the polyphenols in the foods and the calorie-restricting technique employed at the beginning of the diet.

Which foods are allowed to be consumed by someone going through the sirtfood diet? There are a variety of foods that contain the necessary polyphenols that can help activate the sirtuin genes in the body when eating in appropriate quantities. Fruits, vegetables, fish, and other plant-based foods have been touted for years as the keys to weight loss and good health. While most of these foods contain essential nutrients such as vitamins, minerals, and proteins needed for disease prevention and optimal health, more often than not, they do not play direct roles in weight loss.

For food to be allowed into a sirtfood diet, it must not contradict the functioning of the sirtfoods. This means that most plant-based foods, fresh fruits and vegetables, and fish are allowed. However, there are a couple of specific foods that form the core of the sirtfood diet. These foods include, and their active polyphenols include:

Sirtfood	Active Polyphenol
1. Arugula	Quercetin, Kaempferol
2. Buckwheat	Rutin
3. Capers	Kaempferol, Quercetin
4. Celery	Apigenin, Luteolin
5. Chilies	Luteolin, Myricetin
6. Cocoa	Epicatechin
7. Coffee	Caffeic Acid
8. Extra virgin olive oil	Oleuropin, hyroxytyrosol
9. Garlic	Myricetin, Ajoene
10. Green tea	Epicallocatechin gallate
11. Kale	Kaempferol, Quercetin
12. Medjool dates	Caffeic acid, Gallic acid
13. Parsley	Apigenin, Myricetin
14. Red endive	Luteolin

15. Red onion	Quercetin
16. Red wine	Resveratrol
17. Soy	
Formononentin	
18. Strawberries	Fisetin
19. Turmeric	Curcumin
20. Walnuts	Gallic acid

If you hope to achieve any reasonable results with the sirtfood diet, it is also critical that you avoid some foods completely. These foods are going to affect the efficiency of the action of the sirtuin genes and basically work against your progress. These foods include:

1. Alcohols: With the exception of red wine, you need to steer clear of all kinds of alcoholic drinks as you take a step to begin your sirtfood diet journey. Whiskey, brandy, rum, vodka, beer, scotch, tequila, and martinis need to be laid off. Gently adopt the sophisticated practice of drinking red wine instead.

2. Saturated fats: Foods that contain red meat, hot dogs, sausages, and other foods that contain saturated fats shouldn't be eaten if you hope for optimal results from the sirtfood diet.

3. Refined carbohydrates and processed sugar: Foods in this group have little fiber, and the body finds it difficult to digest them. The sugar tends to go straight into the bloodstream as glucose, raising the levels of insulin, the hormone that aids to control

blood sugar. The secretion of insulin, in turn, leads to the inefficient breakdown of stored fats. This is why consistent consumption of processed sugar leads to the accumulation of fats in the body. So, if your body is trying to get rid of your excess fat stores and you keep piling up the fat even more, then you would be rendering the activities of the polyphenols in the sirtfoods ineffective. Foods such as potato chips, French fries, hash brownies, white bread, pasta, and crackers need to be let go of.

Sugary snacks such as candy, ice cream, pastries, cakes, cookies, and muffins also need to be actively avoided. Still on trying to cut down on your sugar consumption, avoiding sweetened drinks such as soda and fruit juices is also important for your enhanced progress with the sirtfood diet.

It's not all gloom and doom, however. You still get to relish coffee, dark chocolate, and of course, red wine as a regular part of your diet while doing your body a great deal of good.

Sirtfoods' edge over other diets

We have extensively gone over the mode of action of sirtfoods and the foods that possess the ability to activate the sirtuin genes. However, what exactly gives sirtfoods the edge over other forms of dieting out there? The simple answers are sustainability and multiple positive effects.

First, one among the most critical downsides of almost all

dieting programs around the world is the problem of calorie restriction. Most diets work on the basis of instructing people to eat certain foods in very strict rations while telling them to stay completely away from almost all the foods they used to love previously. This is placing two huge strains on the individual at once. Not only does he have to let go of his favorite sugary junk food that he's probably been hooked on for years, but he also has to eat new, rather bland food in very little quantities that end up making him hungry. And he has to do that for the rest of this life? How does this plan sound? It sounds completely ridiculous, but it exactly what a lot of dietitians out there expect patients to abide by.

Needless to say, forcing people to give up their sugary treats and eat vegetables twice a day while frantically calculating their calorie intake and freaking out when they 'mistakenly' eat a candy bar is not a sustainable way to build a healthy lifestyle. The sirtfood diet encourages people to eat reasonable portions of healthy food. Sure, in phase 1, the calorie intake per day is restricted to ensure the activation of the Sirtuin genes, but once that phase is over, participants can go back to eating stable, healthy meals without the fear of exceeding any constraining calorie restrictions. This technique helps people to stay satiated and energized, thereby reducing their cravings for the unhealthy foods they used to indulge in. So, the sirtfood diet is more sustainable and reduces the chances of a person relapsing back into their old unhealthy eating habit, and this makes it a very effective option over other diets.

The fact that the sirtfood diet promotes the consumption of healthier food rather than the consumption of less food altogether makes it an amazing contributor to the strength of an individual's immune system. The human immune system is immensely influenced by the quality of the food that an individual eats. Nutritious food substances such as those that make up the sirtfood diet contain natural chemical substances that aid the body's natural defense system. When these food substances are consumed in ample amounts that ensure satiety, they contribute a lot of helpful natural chemical substances to the body, thereby helping to reduce the chances of an individual developing a life-threatening ailment. Calorie-restricting diets, on the other hand, however, prevent the individual from consuming the amount of food that the body needs, thereby cutting down on the amount of significant natural chemicals that the immune system requires for optimal function.

Another point in favor of the sirtfood diet, as opposed to other diets, is the fact that it promotes the abundance of energy, strength, and muscle mass in an individual. As we've severally reiterated, the sirtfood diet actually encourages people to eat healthy food that promotes muscle gain and reduces the accumulation of fats. This simple phenomenon gives the sirtfood diet a great edge over most other diets that focus mainly on restricting calorie intake. The fact that sirtfoods can be eaten until proper satiation is achieved means that people can actually stay energized and strong to tackle their daily goals while gradually building up their muscle mass over time. Most other diets prevent people from eating enough at all, leading to drastic losses in muscle mass, dipping energy levels, and poor physical strength.

To wrap up this exhaustive expose on the sirtfoods and their functioning, let's look at a quick recap of how sirtfoods function and why they are so effective.

Sirtfoods, once again, are a group of foods that contain a specialized group of chemicals known as polyphenols. The polyphenols, in conjunction with the restriction of calories in the first phase of the diet have the unique capability to activate a specialized stress pathway within the body system, which leads to the activation of the inducible sirtuin genes. The sirtuins, once activated, begin to direct a variety of important body-repair processes, which include the burning of fat deposits to provide ample energy for the body, the repair and rejuvenation of body cells, and the strengthening of the body's immune system. Important plant-based foods such as arugula, kale, turmeric, strawberries, red wine, cocoa, soy, red onions, and parsley form essential components of the sirtfood diet due mainly to their ample polyphenol contents.

CHAPTER THREE
SIRTFOOD DIET PHASE 1

N ow that you fully understand what the sirtfood diet is, how it works, and the immense benefits that you can reap from this nutritional regimen, it is time for us to begin to gradually explore the nitty-gritty of the implementation process. How exactly are you supposed to eat the foods that make up the diet?

The first stage of the sirtfood is known as the first phase, or more commonly, 'Phase 1'. Phase 1 is basically the first seven days of the sirtfood diet regimen. Phase 1 is the most intense phase of the sirtfood diet as it is the only phase where you cannot consume above a specified number of calories. In the first three days of phase 1, the maximum permissible number of calories that can be consumed per day is one thousand. In the last four days, the maximum permissible number of consumable calories moves up to 1500. The ambition of the first phase of the sirtfood diet is to help you hit the ground running and activate your sirtuin genes. The restricted number of calories will aid in the activation of your body's stress pathways, which would eventually, together with the action other polyphenols in the sirtfoods, lead to the activation of the sirtuin genes.

At the conclusive end of the first phase, the average mass of fat that would be lost should be between 5 to 7 pounds. However, your body is most likely going to retain all of its muscle or even add up some more, so using a weighing scale to judge the progress of phase 2 might not be such a good idea. So, phase 1 is basically the first seven days of your sirtfood diet.

How do you prepare for phase 1?

When you start out on the sirtfood diet, you are preparing to begin a journey to a new kind of freedom and liberation — freedom from your self-imposed shackles of poor eating habits into a world where you have control over what goes in your body. To get started out for phase 1, you will need to put a couple of things in place. These include:

- A juicer: A lot of modern households already use a juicer in one way or the other on a fairly regular basis. The juicer would be used in the preparation of the sirtfood green juice, a natural concoction of herbs that would help detoxify your body and get you started on dissolving those fatty deposits. Since the aim of the juicer is to extract as much liquid as possible from vegetables, be sure to get one that is better equipped for the type of food products you would be putting in it.

- Secondly, you would need to get familiar with your sirtfood menu and see where exactly you can get all these foods in your neighborhood. Depending on your city, you may be able to get all the sirtfoods you need in your local grocery store, or you may need to try shopping in the open market to get some of the vegetables and food items on the list. The point, however, is to get familiar with the foods that will be forming your new regimen and to figure out how you'd be sourcing these foods.

- Thirdly, you need to figure out a means of preserving the foods you'd be purchasing beforehand. If you have steady access to electricity and a refrigerator, it is advised that you shop for three days' worth of vegetable supplies at once, and store the veggies in your fridge for when you need to make your meals. After three days, you'd need another supply of veggies. The three-day limit is set to prevent spoilage of the veggies, which would only affect the quality of your food and the rate of your development.

- It is also pertinent for you to learn how to prepare the foods you would prepare beforehand. The sirtfood menu features a variety of food options, so it's okay for you to select a few that you can confidently cook right away. As you progress in your journey in the diet, you will gradually learn how to cook more foods and expand your diet.

- Next, it is also critically important for you to plan your eating timetable beforehand. Your sirtfood green juice should be consumed three times per day in the first three days – once when you wake up, thirty minutes to one hour before any meal, and then two other times within the day. Look at your number of calories and plan out when you would be eating and what you would be eating on each day. This will make it an effortless route for you to make these decisions when you finally begin your diet.

- Journaling can be very helpful in helping you stay steadfast on your personal journey. Keeping a journal allows you to keep a chronological record of your struggles and your victories as you go through the sirtfood diet. Journaling on daily basis will not only motivate you to rise up the next day and stick religiously to your diet, but it will also help you to remember how much you have given up to stay healthy and ginger you to keep going when the going gets tough.

- Trying to use the scales to monitor your progress, especially so early into your dieting journey, is a bad idea. As has been repeatedly mentioned, the sirtfood diet helps you to burn fats as well as maintain and even build muscle mass. So as you gear up to begin phase 1 of your diet, try as much as possible to stay off the scales for the meantime and just focus on sticking to this wonderful dieting system.

- Finally, get excited about the journey ahead. To accomplish this, it helps if you can figure out exactly why you are embarking on the sirtfood diet. Are you doing it to reduce your risk of contracting a dangerous lifeothreatening disease along the line? Are you doing it to enhance your career in the media or modeling industry? Are you doing it to improve your mental health and improve your moods, focus, and concentration? Whatever be your reason for wanting to make the important personal sacrifice of starting up the sirtfood diet, remind yourself that you are finally about to achieve those aims. Be excited that your life is about to experience a positive turn around.

Expectations for Phase 1

You may wonder – what exactly is Phase 1 going to entail, and what results can I expect to achieve after the first week of my diet? With great sacrifice, they say, comes great rewards. Phase 1 is going to be the most tasking phase of your diet, no doubt, but it will also be the phase that provides you with the most pleasantly surprising results. At the end of phase 1, you can expect to lose between 5 to 7 pounds of weight in pure fat, as evidenced by the results of the cohort study carried out in London. You can also expect to experience enhanced mental clarity and focus, and a general feeling of lightness and agility.

However, since phase 1 is going to be your stage of making the most important sacrifices for future benefits, it also means you would probably have to deal with some discomfort during this phase. Not everybody would experience these signs, but some participants in the diet have reported feelings of hunger, lethargy, slight irritability, and even strong cravings for junk food and sugary snacks and drinks during the first phase. It is believed that the restriction of the calories consumed by the participant in the first three days to one thousand calories, and to fifteen hundred calories in the last four days of phase one is responsible for these challenges.

So, if you feel really hungry, tired, or extremely desirous of junk food during your first phase, be patient. Remember your reason for starting this, and renew your resolve to stay strong and fight for the dazzling life you've dreamed of every single day. Usually, in the final days of phase one, as your body gets used to the diet, you will feel your fatigue and tiredness slipping away, and these feelings would become replaced by feelings of strength, clarity, and agility. As you switch from one thousand calories to fifteen hundred calories per day, you will feel more satiated and energized too, and your moods will generally improve. From this point onwards, your journey becomes progressively easier.

Meal plan for Phase 1

For the first three days of the sirtfood diet, you will be expected to drink three sirtfood juices and eat one mail sirtfood meal per day. This combination helps to keep the number of calories consumed just under one thousand. For the last four days of the first phase, however, you will be required to eat two main sirtfood meals and two sirtfood juices on a daily basis. This combination would sum up to about fifteen hundred calories.

As you can probably already predict, the sirtfood green juice would be an essential part of your sirtfood diet in phase one and beyond. After water, this drink would constitute a major percentage of your total fluid intake as you proceed with the sirtfood diet. Other fluids that you would be permitted to consume would include black coffee (i.e., without milk) and green tea. Milk should be abstained from during the first phase of the sirtfood diet as it contains active substances that may hamper the activation of the sirtuin genes.

Since the sirtfood green juice is so critical to the success of your sirtfood diet, let's examine exactly how to make the sirtfood green juice before delving into what your model meal plan should look like.

To prepare the sirtfood green juice, you'll need:

- 2.5 oz. kale

- 1 oz. arugula

- 0.25 oz. flat-leaf parsley

- 5.5 oz. celery stalks (with leaves)

- 0.5 medium green apple

- 1 in. ginger

- Half of a lemon, squeezed or juiced.

- 0.5 tsp. matcha powder

Note that the matcha powder should only be included only in the first two juices of the day during the first three days of phase one. Basically, between day 1 and 3, only the juice you'd be drinking very early in the morning before breakfast, and the drink you'll be having by midmorning should contain matcha. Your third sirtfood juice of the day should not contain matcha powder because the substance has been found to be caffeinated and may alter your sleep pattern if taken too late in the day. So, do not forget – no matcha for the last juice of the day between days 1 and 3.

For the final four days of phase one, however, it is okay to put matcha powder in the two sirtfood juices you'll be drinking daily. This is because you'd have completed your daily required sirtfood juice intake by midday, provided you follow the laid-down guidelines.

So, now that you know the ingredients and you know the sirtfood juice rules let's get into the nitty-gritty of making this wonderfully wholesome drink.

- First of all, mix your veggies in the juicer. This means your arugula, kale, and parsley should be loaded into the juicer. Ensure to extract as much fluid as possible from these greens to ensure that you get maximum value for your time, effort, and money. After the juicing process, you should have obtained about a quarter of a cup of veggie juice. Absolutely delicious, yeah?

- The next step is to lead your apples, ginger, and celery into the juicer and extract the fluid from those too. Add this new mixture to the one obtained in the first step.

- Next, peel your lemon, cut it in half, and squeeze out the juice. If you feel that your squeezing is not efficient enough, you can use the juicer instead. After adding the lemon juice to your mixture, you should have about a cup of juice ready.

- Pour out a small portion of your juice and add in your half teaspoon of matcha powder. Ensure that the matcha dissolves properly in the juice, and then pour the matcha-containing juice into the rest of the juice.

- Stir your juice properly, and you may add a little water to adjust the taste if you like. Enjoy the immaculate taste of good health!

Now that you have gotten a good grasp of how to make your sirtfood green juice, it's time to design a workable meal plan that would allow you to access a variety of sirtfoods to aid your progress in phase 1. Remember that in each day for your first three days, you must drink a cup of sirtfood green juice thrice, and eat a sirtfood main meal once. For the remaining four days of Phase 1, its two sirtfood juices and two main meals to give fifteen hundred calories.

Let's break the meal plan down now.

- Day 1: Sirtfood green juice – 3 times

Main meal – 1 time

Meal idea: Stir-fried Asian shrimp, buckwheat noodles and dark chocolate (85% cocoa)

Vegan option: Sesame glazed tofu, miso, ginger, chili, stir-fried greens, and dark chocolate (85% cocoa).

- Day 2: Sirtfood green juice – 3 times

Main meal: 1 time

Meal idea: Aromatic chicken breast, kale, red onions, tomato, and chili salsa

Vegan option: Kale, red onion dal, and buckwheat.

- Day 3: Sirtfood green juice – 3 times

Main meal: 1 time

Meal idea: Turkey escalope, capers, sage, parsley, cauliflower, and dark chocolate.

Vegan option: Baked tofu, cauliflower, and dark chocolate.

From day four onwards, you can eat ½ oz. Dark chocolate once a day, preferably alongside one meal.

- Day 4: Sirtfood green juice – 2 times

Main meal: 2 times

Meal 1: Sirt muesli

Meal 2: Salmon fillet, endive, arugula, and celery salad.

Vegan option 1: Sirt muesli

Vegan option 2: Tuscan bean stew.

- Day 5: Sirtfood green juice – 2 times

Main meal: 2 times

Meal 1 (Vegan and regular diets): Sirt super salad.

Meal 2 (regular diet): Grilled beef, red wine, onion rings, garlic, kale, and roasted potatoes.

Meal 2 (Vegan diet): Kidney bean mole and baked potatoes.

- Day 6: Sirtfood green juice – 2 times

Main meal: 2 times

Meal 1: Sirtfood omelet

Meal 2: Baked chicken breast, parsley pesto, red onion salad.

Vegan option 1: Waldorf salad.

Vegan option 2: Roasted eggplants, walnuts, parsley pesto, and tomato salad.

- Day 7: Sirtfood green juice – 2 times

Main meal: 2 times

Meal 1: Strawberry buckwheat salad

Meal 2: Baked cod marinated in miso, sesame, and stir-fried greens

Vegan option 1: Strawberry buckwheat salad.

Vegan option 2: Buckwheat noodles in miso broth, tofu, celery, and kale.

CHAPTER FOUR
SIRTFOOD DIET PHASE 2

What is Phase 2?

In the previous chapter, we extensively described what Phase 1 of the sirtfood diet is. After successfully completing the first seven days of the sirtfood diet, then you would be starting Phase 2 on the 8th day. Phase 2 simply refers to a two-week period after the first seven days of the sirtfood diet. Phase two is a nutrient-packed 14-day period that allows you to raise your calorie consumption while integrating the sirtfood diet into your usual daily routine.

In phase 2 of the sirtfood diet, it is expected that you would progress with your fat loss. As phase 2 progresses, if you stick religiously with your diet, you are likely to find yourself getting slimmer and feeling even more energized and pumped to tackle your daily tasks. In phase 2 of the sirtfood diet, you would be eating three times a day, meaning that issues of hunger, fatigue, and irritability due to restriction of calories should not be a problem here. Even though it is advised that you eat thrice, it is still recommended that you do not over-eat. Eat till you feel reasonably full and satisfied, and then stop. Satisfaction and sustainability are the hallmarks of phase 2, and this phase, if handled well, will help you integrate the sirtfood diet into your lifestyle.

How to Prepare for Phase 2

To help you coast through the second phase of the sirtfood diet successfully, there are trifling pointers that you harmonize and probably start implementing right from your first phase. These tips include:

- Rise early: As we have mentioned in the previous chapter, the sirtfood green juice remains a crucial and critical part of your diet. To ensure that you maximize the benefits of this power drink, it is important that you drink it thirty minutes to one hour before having your main breakfast. Waking up early will help you ensure that you drink your sirtfood green juice, get a little workout done, and get ready for work before finally eating your healthy sirtfood breakfast. The combination of the sirtfood meal and the sirtfood green juice will help fill you up and get you energized to maximize your day, while of course, helping you to melt away those fat deposits along the way.

- Eat dinner early: Whether you are on a diet or not, medical experts generally advise against late-might eating. It is healthier to eat your dinner early, between 6 PM and 7 PM, and then get a little rest before retiring to bed. So, instead of working late and wolfing down a heavy dinner in bed at 11 PM, try to take a break, eat your healthy dinner, and then get back to handling the rest of your work. It helps if you are done with your work at least one hour before bed so that you can give your body the opportunity to gradually calm down before you sleep. To ensure the optimal success of the sirtfood diet, you should get an average of 7 -8 hours of sleep per night. If you are extremely busy, try to get at least 6 hours of sleep every night. That will help the nutrients in the food repair and rejuvenate your body cells, which will make you healthier, stronger, and well-built. Sleeping early also generally makes you focused and energized when you wake up to tackle the challenges of the next day.

- Eat balanced, measured potions: It is important to strike a balance in the quantity of food you would be eating. Eat too much, and you would be overloading your body with calories. You may think: "But the aim is to get as much of the important chemicals as possible!". Yes, you want to have as many polyphenols as healthily possible into your system, but over-eating can cause constipation and affect the action of the sirtuins in your body. So, eat till you are satiated, and then stop. Since you will be eating three meals per day in the second phase, there is no need for you to overload yourself at any time. Eat till you feel reasonably satisfied, get to work, and then eat another meal later. You don't have to go hungry, but you don't have to overload yourself to the point of lethargy either. Let your appetite guide you and stay energized and focused.

- Drink your sirtfood juice once: The sirtfood juice is an excellent source of nutrients and polyphenols for activating your sirtuin genes. However, as you progress with the diet and eat more food on a daily basis, you are required to gradually begin to slow down your consumption of the sirtfood green juice., You will recall that in Phase 1, the sirtfood green juice was recommended to be consumed thrice per day alongside one mail for the first three days. In the last four days of phase 1, the recommended daily intake of the sirtfood green juice reduces to two cups, and you become required to eat two meals per day. Once you transition into phase 2 of your diet, however, things change. You can now eat three meals per day, meaning you can get an optimum supply of your nutrients from your food, and intense calorie restriction is no longer necessary. For this reason, once phase 2 begins, you should only consume your sirtfood green juice only once a day – and that's very early in the morning, thirty minutes to one hour before your main breakfast.

Apart from the sirtfood green juice, you can still drink a couple of liquids in phase 2 of the diet. These liquids include water, flavored water, black coffee, and green tea. You may also consume red wine up to three times a week as soon as you commence phase 2.

Expectations for Phase 2

In phase 2, your weight loss journey will continue. The amount of fat that would be eradicated in this phase would vary from one individual to another. However, it is not unconventional for people to lose up to 10 more pounds in pure fat in this phase. As we constantly advise, do not try to judge the success of your dieting efforts by checking a weighing scale every morning. The diet is aimed to help you burn fat and improve your muscle mass, so while losing fat, your muscle cells may be actively dividing, thereby helping you to increase your muscle mass. To help you track your fat loss rate, you can look at your body periodically in the mirror, check the fit of your clothes, or ask for a few trusted opinions.

Phase 2 will also come with enhanced focus and vitality. The active components of the sirtfoods will continue to keep your sirtuin genes activated, leading to feelings of enhanced mental clarity and boosted concentration. The consumption of the foods contained in the sirtfood diet helps to rejuvenate your brain cells, thereby helping to improve brainpower.

If you were addicted to junk food and sugary products prior to staring the sirtfood diet, phase 2 is the stage where your cravings begin to lessen considerably. This is because you would be having three healthy meals per day, and a nutrient-packed cup of green juice to start your day with. Your body would constantly feel satiated, and that urge to dash across the street to grab a burger and a soda just won't be there since you would not be feeling hungry in the first place.

In the long-term, completing phase 2 of the sirtfood diet and moving on to integrate the sirtfood diet system into your lifestyle would help reduce your susceptibility to debilitating diseases. The consumption of unhealthy food leads to the accumulation of fat deposits in the body, as has been described earlier in this book. When you consume a lot of sugar processed regularly, the sugar will gain easy access to your bloodstream, increasing your blood sugar levels, and by extension, your insulin levels. Once your insulin levels pass a certain safe threshold, the natural burning of fats in the body is suppressed, and you begin to trend towards obesity. With obesity comes a high likelihood of heart disease since the fats would make it compulsory for the heart to pump blood at unhealthily high pressure. In some cases, the fat deposits may even block key blood vessels within the body, which can lead to falling unconscious and even death.

Meal Plan for Phase 2

Throughout the fourteen days of phase 2, you will be drinking one serving of sirtfood juice very early in the morning at least thirty minutes to one hour before food. You will also be consuming three standard meals a day – breakfast, lunch, and dinner. These meals will provide your body with the necessary calories and nutrients it needs to stay energized and satiated while eradicating unhealthy fat deposits and repairing your body's cells. In phase 2, carefully selected sirtfood snacks may also be introduced, and they may be consumed once or twice per day. The sirtfood snacks can particularly come in handy when you are in a position where you cannot have a standard meal right away. So instead of violating your diet's rules and eating unhealthy junk, you can simply have a healthy sirtfood snack, pending the time you can eat a standard meal. Sirtfood snacks can be particularly great for long meetings, flights, and long road travels, shopping, and other related circumstances.

Also, one final reminder, the sirtfood diet works best when the foods digest and get the chance to start working before you go to bed, so your dinner should not exceed 7 PM.

Breakfast Options

The foods in this section may be eaten at 7-day intervals. Depending on your preferences and your schedule, however, you can modify this suggestion to fit your lifestyle. Meal option one may be eaten on the eighth day of your diet and the 15th day, for instance. Meal 2 may be eaten on day 9 of the diet and day 16. The point is to make the food as varied as possible and to eat as many meals as possible before consuming the same food again.

The breakfast options include:

1. Sirtfood smoothie

2. Sirt muesli

3. Yogurt, berries, walnut and dark chocolate

4. Spicy scrambled eggs

5. Mushroom/ tofu scramble

6. Buckwheat pancakes, walnuts, strawberries and chocolate

7. Sirtfood omelet.

Lunch options

Just as instructed for the breakfast options, the lunch options may also be eaten once a week, preferably on a specific day of the week to help you vary your diet and find your new feeding regimen interesting. Lunch options include:

1. Sirt chicken salad.
2. Waldorf salad – apples, walnuts, celery, and mayonnaise.
3. Sirt tuna salad.
4. Strawberry buckwheat salad.
5. Buckwheat pasta salad.
6. Tofu and shiitake mushroom soup
7. Whole wheat leavened bread.

Dinner options

Foods that may be eaten for dinner during phase 2 of the sirtfood diet include:

1. Stir-fry shrimp and buckwheat noodles.
2. Tuscan bean stew.

3. Potatoes, kale, curry, and chicken.
4. Kale, red onions and buckwheat
5. Sirt chili con carne
6. Kidney bean mole and baked potatoes
7. Sirtfood pizza.

CHAPTER FIVE
GETTING STARTED: YOUR SHOPPING LIST

Now that you fully understand what the first and second phases of the sirtfood diet entail, it is high time you took another step towards actualizing your dreams of morphing into your dream figure and improving your overall physical and mental health. In this chapter, we would be looking at the twenty essential food items that make up the core of the sirtfood diet, why these foods are so important to the journey you are about to undertake, and how much these foods are likely to cost. As we journey through this chapter, you would notice that a lot of the core sirtfoods are vegetables. Hence, you can easily purchase them at the produce section of your local grocery store. Where possible, it is important that you purchase these food items in their natural state instead of in their processed form. However, some of these foods are going to have to be processed, so we would be looking at the best possible brands whose composition would allow you to achieve the best possible results for your dieting efforts.

The foods that are listed in this section do not form an exhaustive list of foods that have the power to activate the powerful sirtuin genes. There are several other foods, most of them, fruits, vegetables, and whole grains that have considerable levels of polyphenols, which have significant effects on weight loss and cell rejuvenation too. However, the top twenty sirtfoods have been proven by research to be the most important sirtfoods discovered to date. Hence, we would be closely examining each of these sirtfoods in this chapter. You would be using most of these foods to prepare your meals during phase 1 and phase 2 and beyond, so we would be examining the prices of these food products, their individual health benefits, and recommended brands in cases where you can get pure organic fresh produce.

Berries are a family of foods outside the top twenty sirtfoods that have significant polyphenol contents within them. Strawberries are part of the top 20 sirtfoods, and they contain enormous amounts of Fisetin, an important polyphenol that has important antioxidative and anti-carcinogenic properties. While strawberries are core sirtfoods, other berries also contain varying concentrations of other important polyphenols and can be ingested as a part of the sirtfood diet too. Blackberries, blackcurrants, blueberries and raspberries are not essential sirtfoods, nut they can help significantly on your journey to weight loss and enhanced physical and mental health.

Nuts are another group of foods with one essential representative in the top twenty sirtfoods, but with other members packing different levels of important polyphenols. Walnuts are core sirtfoods, due to the high concentration of Gallic acid in them. Chestnuts, pecans, pistachios, and peanuts, however, also contain other important biochemicals that have neem proven to be helpful with fat loss and reducing the risk of chronic diseases. You have to be extremely heedful when it comes to consuming nuts, however, as specific individuals may have allergies to nuts. Peanut allergies are particularly common in the United States.

Whole grains are also important foods that can immense health impacts by helping individuals lose unhealthy fat deposits and prevent the development of chronic diseases. Whole grains contain a high content of sirtuin activators; however, once the grains are processed and become white, most of the essential nutrients get stripped off during the refining process. Therefore, all processed grain gives you is pure carbohydrate, which you don't want too much of is you are trying to lose weight. If you stick with whole grains such as unprocessed wheat and rice, you are likely to reap a lot of important health benefits than if you choose the processed versions of these foods. The pleasant news is that if you are trying to stay gluten-free, you can find the perfect gluten-free whole grain options for you at most grocery stores near you. If you are also looking to indulge in a healthy snack every now and them, popcorn serves as a great way of keeping you filled while making sure that you do not fill your body up with unhealthy carbohydrates.

Now, let's get into your shopping list properly. Here are the top twenty sirtfoods that you should purchase as basics as you prepare to start up your sirtfood diet:

1. Dark Chocolate: Let's start with something fun, shall we? Chocolate has always been an all-time favorite among adults and children alike all over the world. There are quite a number of chocolate types, however, and chocolate is usually classified based on the percentage of the various constituents it contains. Milk chocolate bars are quite popular in the US and other parts of the world, but as we mentioned earlier in this book, the aim is to keep your milk consumption as low as possible, since milk tends to interfere with the activation of the sirtuin genes. The specific type of chocolate that is best for this diet is dark chocolate. This chocolate variety should contain an optimal 85% of cocoa, with the remaining 15%$ being a mix of other constituents. Dark chocolate's extremely high cocoa content makes it a rich source of the polyphenol Epicatechin, which functions in helping to lower blood pressure by removing any fatty instructions in the body's vascular system.

As we have reviewed earlier, one of the major causes of high blood pressure is the presence of numerous fatty deposits in the major blood vessels of the body, making it pertinent for the heart to pump blood with more pressure to get the needed blood to all parts of the body. By helping to clear the fat deposits in the blood vessels, the long-term consumption of Epicatechin in dark cocoa helps improve cardiac health and vascular function in the body. Epicatechin has also been proven to greatly boost cognitive function. The polyphenol has the ability to help boost cell division rate and slow down cell damage in the brain, thereby helping to improve an individual's cognitive abilities, including memory and information processing functions. Cocoa has also been proven to aid in the protection of the skin from the harmful ultraviolet rays of the sun.

While shopping for your dark chocolate, it is extremely important to look out for brands that have undergone an alkalization process called 'dutching.' This process is used mainly for preserving the chocolate, but it affects the concentration of the polyphenols that we need in our chocolate. Dark chocolate contains a low sugar content, meaning that it would help you relish the inimitable taste of chocolate without flooding your body with unhealthy processed sugar. Dark chocolate also contains fewer additives and preservatives that can affect the positive effects of the polyphenols contained within it. Including dark chocolate as a regular feature in your diet can help curb your sugar cravings and boost the endorphin and serotonin levels in your brain, thereby helping to greatly improve your mood, eradicate irritability and fatigue, and help you stay focused and motivated for longer periods of time.

Recommended brands of dark chocolate that you can shop online or in a local store near you include Endangered Species Dark Chocolate, Alter Eco Dark Chocolate, Taza Dark Chocolate, and Lindt Dark Chocolate. You can obtain packs of these dark chocolate brands from between $15 to $40, depending on your outlet and preferred brand.

2. Red Wine: A lot of people who know a thing or two about the sirtfood diet know that the inclusion of red wine in this diet is one of its most enjoyable parts. Red wine contains a considerably high amount of antioxidants and anti-inflammatory agents. Red wine contains high concentrations of resveratrol, one of the first polyphenols ever discovered. Resveratrol has also been proven to promote healthy aging and prevent various types of cancers. Red wine's high resveratrol content enables it to help prevent the formation of blood clots within your blood vessels. As some individuals age, due to the lack of necessary thinning agents in their blood, possibly due to an unhealthy diet or due to genetics, blood clots may form within their vascular system. If these blood clots happen to block blood flow to a critical organ like the brain, the person might die a

sudden, painful death. A glass of red wine a day, possibly with your last meal of the day can be a very great addition to your diet.

Recommended brands of red wine include the Oak Leaf Vineyards Cabernet Sauvignon Red Wine and the Franzia Cabernet Red Wine. You can obtain a bottle of these wines under $20 at a local store near you.

3. Red Onions: While onions have a reputation for being one of the world's most popular food flavoring agents, not much is usually discussed about this superfood's incredible immune-system boosting properties. Red onions have high concentrations of the polyphenol Quercetin, antioxidants, and Vitamin C, making this food a powerhouse capable of preventing a wide variety of diseases from cancers to heart diseases. The antioxidants in e=red onions okay vital roles in helping to reverse the effects of free radicals, which can lead to damaged cells and accelerated aging. Onions may also play important roles in accelerating the healing of internal and external wounds such as ulcers. Red onions generally have a low amount of calories, making them a valuable addition to the sirtfood diet. You can purchase fresh red onions from your local produce store at under $2 per pound.

4. Green Tea: Tea is one of the most popular beverages in the world. In ancient Asian civilizations, tea was

considered a culturally significant drink because of its recognized healing and calming properties. Green tea contains a specific polyphenol compound known as Epicatechin gallate. This polyphenol plays a very important role in weight loss. If you remember the description of the process for making the sirtfood green juice, you'd recall that matcha (a form of green tea) was required to be included in the juice because of its superior fat-burning abilities. Green tea contains a superb concentration of antioxidants that play essential roles in helping to prevent the body's cells from the damage caused by free radicals. Green tea has also been proven to boost metabolic rates, thereby improving the rate of digestion and absorption of food into the body. High metabolic rates would help get you energized faster and will keep you going for longer.

Green tea is very useful, it has also been proven, based on research, to help prevent and mitigate inflammations in the body. Green tea's polyphenol content also enables this fantastic beverage to play a key role in the prevention of heart and brain disorders. By helping to rapidly burn the fat deposits within the body, green tea can help prevent heart diseases in the long-term. By aiding the rapid repair and rejuvenation of the brain cells, green tea helps to promote long-term brain health and helps to boost cognitive functions in the short term.

Recommended brands of green tea include Celestial Seasonings Green Tea and Great Value Green Tea. Most green tea packs can be purchased between $10 to $15 in the US.

5. Coffee: Once again, we have another popular American beverage. Coffee has grown to become an indispensable part of the lives of billions of people around the world, from professionals in the corporate world to entrepreneurs and academics. Coffee is renowned for its stimulating and relaxing abilities and is usually consumed in the morning and early in the afternoon. The chances that you drink coffee, at least on a fairly regular basis already, is quite high. However, as you transition into the sirtfood diet, it is important that you understand that you would now be required to take your coffee black (i.e., without milk and preferably without processed sugar). Black coffee enables you to experience the distinctive flavor of coffee in all its glory and offers your body with astonishing health benefits.

Coffee has been known to give the body a sharp energy boost, helping a lot of people to stay alert early in the day. Coffee has also been proven to significantly improve brain function in the short-term and long-term. Caffeic acid is the active polyphenol on coffee, and this amazing biochemical has been proven to burn fat deposits on the body, thereby helping to lower the risk of a variety of diseases extending from Type 2 diabetes to heart disease. Coffee's brain stimulating properties make it a great preventive food against cognitive deficiencies such as Alzheimer's, dementia, and Parkinson's disease. The regular consumption of coffee has also been proven to help fight cancer depression and liver damage.

Recommended coffee brands for you to start off your coffee diet include Folger's Classic Roast, Maxwell House Light Roast, and McCafe Light Roast Coffee. These coffee brands can be purchased online or at a local store near you between $15 to $20.

Arugula: Arugula is one of the powerful green vegetables in the sirtfood diet, and is undoubtedly one of the most nutritionally beneficial foods among the top twenty sirtfoods. Arugula has been proven to help boost weight loss due to the presence of the essential polyphenols – quercetin and Kaempferol present in this vegetable. Arugula is loaded with a variety of essential nutrients ranging from Calcium which can help strengthen bones and teeth, Potassium which aids nervous coordination and brain function, Folate which is extremely critical to fetal development in pregnant women, Vitamin C which helps to boost the power of the immune system, and Vitamin K which aids in blood coagulation to prevent hemorrhage in the case of an injury.

Arugula's important polyphenols play huge roles in the

repair and rejuvenation of damaged brain cells. This helps to prevent the brains of aging people from rapid cognitive decline. Arugula also boosts bone strength, helps remove harmful toxins from the body system, and has been found to exhibit important anti-inflammatory effects in the body. Since arugula is a green vegetable, it is best to buy it fresh and unpackaged. You can get a pound of arugula from your local grocery's produce section below $15 per pound.

6. Buckwheat: Buckwheat is an important core sirtfood of Asian origins that features the polyphenol Rutin. Buckwheat can significantly lower the body's cholesterol levels, thereby helping to decrease the risk of heart disease in the long term. Buckwheat also plays important roles in helping to lower the blood sugar level, thereby instigating a decrease in the body's insulin levels too, thereby decreasing the risk of type 2 diabetes and making the fat loss process significantly easier. Buckwheat is extremely rich in dietary fibers, which aid digestion and prevent constipation and flatulence. Buckwheat is rich in proteins and can help play important roles in the prevention and retardation of cancerous growths.

Recommended buckwheat brands include Arrowhead Mills Organic Buckwheat Groats and Bob's Red Mill Organic Buckwheat Groats. You can get a can of buckwheat groats between $10 and $15, depending on your location.

7. Capers: A caper is a flower-bud gotten from a very specific shrub that is said to have originated from Southern Europe. Capers contain the important polyphenols Rutin and Quercetin, which both aid in cell rejuvenation and the prevention of internal inflammations within the body system. Capers have significant percentages of antioxidants that play vital roles in counteracting the oxidative effects of free radicals on the body's organs. Free radicals may be generated by eating some of the more harmful conventional foods we eat, and they may hasten the aging process, leading to the breakdown of essential tissues and organs, and hasten the onset of chronic diseases. Antioxidants in capers, however, play important roles in helping to wipe out these free radicals. Capers also promote the smooth circulation of blood in the body. When blood vessels are blocked by fat deposits, the heart would need to pump blood at a higher pressure, a situation that can lead to high blood pressure. In some situations, the blood supply to important extremities may be cut off. Eating capers and other sirtfood greens can help to constantly clean up the vascular system and prevent blood circulation problems. Capers are also loaded with essential macronutrients such as

Calcium which supports strong bones and teeth, Iron that promotes the retention of oxygen in the blood, copper which serves as a catalyst for many of the body's natural biochemical processes, and sodium which is critical to the proper functioning of the body's nervous system.

Capers have also been found to help mitigate issues related to indigestion and constipation. This is because capers have relatively high fiber content, and fibers have the ability to smoothen and quicken body metabolism. The regular consumption of capers may also help prevent rheumatism, diabetes, low blood sugar, and skin problems.

If you can obtain fresh capers in your local store, then that would be wonderful. However, if you can't, you can count on trusted brands such as Paesana Non-Pareil Capers, and San Antonio Non-Pareil Capers. The 32oz. Packs of both sell for just under $20.

8. Celery: Celery is a vegetable that has become an indispensable part of most American diets; therefore, it is hardly a food that needs a lot of introduction. Celery, when consumed together with its leaves, is quite rich in a lot of essential vitamins and minerals. Apart from helping with the activation of your sirtuin genes, and by extension, weight loss and optimum well-being, celery furnishes your body with Vitamin K, which helps your blood clot

properly during wounds, Potassium, that aids in nervous coordination, vitamin A that improves your eyesight, and Folate that is exceptive to the comform growth and development of fetuses in the womb.

Celery has also been proven to have antioxidative and anti-inflammatory properties and can help aid digestion. It is advisable to purchase this vegetable from the fresh produce section of your local grocery store. Celery can be purchased at under $3/kilogram.

9. Chilies: Chilies are another spicy American favorite. There are several fast food joints that sell thousands of plates of chili-based foods around the country. However, we still recommend you cook your chili-based meals at home Chilies have the capacity to prevent and manage inflammation, and they help relieve the body from pains. Chilies can also help to improve cardiac health and lessen the chances of you contracting a cardiovascular disease down the line by helping to rid the body of unnecessary fat deposits. Chilies have also been proven to help clear congestion, boost immunity, and of course, burn off fats.

It is recommended that you purchase fresh chili from the produce section of your local grocery. Prices usually range between $2 -$3 per kilogram.

10. Extra Virgin Olive Oil: This essential food product is one of the key constituents of the native Mediterranean diet that makes people from that region so healthy and physically fit. Extra virgin olive oil has a magnificent capacity to burn away fats from the body, thereby helping greatly to reduce the risk of heart disease and helping you to achieve your dream body. Extra virgin olive oil plays important roles in helping to improve blood circulation and removing vascular debris, thereby reducing the chances of a stroke. A stroke occurs when blood flow to the brain is interrupted. However, when extra virgin olive oil is consumed regularly alongside other healthy sirtfoods, most of the vascular debris in your blood vessels would be regularly flushed out, thereby helping to keep your healthier for longer. Due to its spectacular fat-burning abilities, extra virgin olive oil also helps to lower the risk of Type 2 diabetes.

Extra virgin olive oil is also active against cancer-causing agents, and its cell rejuvenation capabilities make it active in the prevention of cognitive decline and the enhancement of memory.

Recommended extra virgin olive oil brands include Great Value 1005 Extra Virgin Olive Oil and Pompeian Smooth Extra Virgin Olive Oil. Both can be purchased between $5 -

$10 per bottle.

11. Garlic: Garlic is a member of the allium family that consists of leeks, shallot, and onions. Garlic contains a high concentration of essential vitamins and minerals that aid the proper functioning of the human body. Garlic is loaded with Vitamin C, which boosts the body's immunity and promotes the healing of wounds and Fibers, which aid with digestion and regent constipation. Due to its ability to efficiently burn up the body's fat deposits without affecting muscle gain, garlic is potent food for bodybuilding and weight loss. Due to its ability to remove harmful cholesterol from the body, garlic is reputable for its role in abbreviating the risk of heart disease in the long term. Garlic also helps to reduce the rate of cell death and promotes the rejuvenation and repair of damaged cells, thereby helping to slow down the aging process.

It is best to buy fresh organic garlic from the produce section of your grocery store. Fresh garlic prices should range around $4 per pound. However, you can also get a 9.5-ounce tin of minced garlic for around $4 too.

12. Kale: Kale is referred to as a superfood by most new-age nutritionists, and it is indeed one of the most richly endowed vegetables available today. Kale has a high concentration if the polyphenols Quercetin

and Kaempferol, thereby helping to burn up body fats and boost natural immunity. Kale's immunity-boosting properties are compounded even further by the presence of Vitamin C, which also helps accelerate the healing of wounds and the presence of antioxidants that play vital roles in counteracting the nocuous effects of free radicals on the body. Kale's high Vitamin K content promotes the clotting of blood, and its ability to remove cholesterol from the body also helps to lessen the chances of heart disease in the long run. Kale has also been reported to contain significant levels of Vitamin A, Vitamin B6, Manganese, Calcium, Copper, Potassium, and Magnesium.

The presence of the biochemical Lutein and Zeaxanthin help in conjunction with kale's significant Vitamin A and Beta carotene to greatly improve eye-sight, and prevent eye disorders in the long term. Like all leafy vegetables, it is advisable to purchase kale fresh from the organic produce section of your local grocery. At $1 per pound, kale is one hell of an affordable magic health potion.

13. Medjool dates: Medjool dates are sweeter, larger, and darker than the regular dates you are likely used to. Medjool dates are not just a tasty treat; they have a high fiber concentration, making them important in healthy, rapid digestion and the prevention of

constipation. Medjool dates prevent heart disease by functioning heavily in the removal of unhealthy fats, and these dates contain a high concentration of antioxidants which retard the activities of free radicals. Medjool dates contain high concentrations of calcium, phosphorus, and magnesium, making them essential in the building and maintenance of strong bones and teeth. Medjool dates have a reasonable carbohydrate content, making them surprisingly powerful sources of energy. Medjool dates are extremely efficient in the invigoration of existing brain cells and the restoration of damaged ones, making them essential for optimum long-term brain health and the prevention of cognitive decline as you age,

At 23 pieces per pound, you can buy a pound of Medjool dates at your local grocery store for about $10.

14. Parsley: Parsley is a green vegetable that is highly consumed among the natives of the Mediterranean region – one of the healthiest regions of the world, by virtue of their uniquely healthy diet. Parsley contains a healthy dose of antioxidants and anticarcinogenic biochemical, which combat the oxidative effects of free radicals, and the tumor-causing effects of carcinogens. Parsley also packs a lot of Lutein, Beta carotene, and Zeaxanthin, making

this core sirtfood extremely helpful in maintaining perfect eyesight and preventing eye defects as the body ages. Parsley's ability to help burn unhealthy fat deposits makes it key to long-term cardiac health, and its anti-bacterial properties make it important in helping the body fight infections. You can easily purchase a pound of parsley at your local grocery at under $6 per pound.

15. Red Endive: This veggie contains Kaempferol, a polyphenol that promotes the burning of fats, and increased cognitive abilities. Red endives are anti-carcinogenic, boost cardiac health, improve vision, and promote optimum fetal development in pregnant women due to their high concentrations of folate. Red endives can be purchased at the fresh produce section of your local grocery store at $2.50 per pound.

16. Soy: Soybeans are one of the world's most prolific legumes in terms of protein content. The huge amount of pure plant protein in soybeans makes them critical to building muscle mass and promoting the restoration and rejuvenation of body cells, Soybeans contain low fat and cholesterol levels and play major roles in helping to reduce the accumulation of unhealthy fat deposits within the body, thereby boosting long-term cardiac health.

Soybeans are also rich in Vitamin K, Folate, Copper Manganese, and Phosphorus. Soybeans have been found to possess strong anti-carcinogenic properties and have biochemicals that help alleviate the symptoms of menopause, thereby helping older women transit painlessly into another phase of their lives. You can buy organic soybeans from your local grocery store at around $15 per pound.

17. Strawberries: Welcome the brightest and most attractive member of the sirtfoods – even though some people might argue that dark chocolate is the most attractive core sirtfood. Soybeans are sweet, juicy and appealing, and contain huge amounts of Vitamin C, making them essential in boosting immunity and promoting the quick healing of internal and external wounds, Soybeans also contain antioxidants, thereby helping to promote healthy aging, and manganese and folate. Because of their fat-burning powers, strawberries can promote long-term cardiac well-being and control blood sugar levels. You can purchase a 2-pound pack of strawberries at your local produce store for just under $4.

18. Turmeric: Turmeric is one of the most respected spices in the world, and for a good reason. Turmeric is a natural anti-inflammatory agent, possesses

natural antioxidants, and is very efficient at reducing an individual's risk of brain disease. Turmeric is as well equipped with the ability to lower the risk of heart disease and cancer. The natural pain-relief agents in turmeric make it important in the mitigation of arthritis and general muscle pains. Turmeric's natural polyphenols also have a general calming effect on the mind, helping to ward off symptoms of clinical depression. You can purchase a pound of ground turmeric at your local store for around $12.

19. Walnuts: Finally, we have our last core sirtfood, and it is definitely one of the most prolific species of nuts to have ever existed. Nuts are generally regarded as powerful foods that help a person lose weight and reduce the risk of chronic diseases. Walnuts, however, also possess powerful antioxidants that counteract the effects of free radicals and reduce an individual's risk of contracting Type 2 diabetes, heart disease, and cancer.

20. Recommended walnut brands include Great Value Chopped Walnut (24 oz.) and Fisher Chef's Natural Walnut Halves and Pieces (32 oz.), both costing about $10 and $13 respectively.

To this conclusive juncture, we have come to the end of your shopping list for phase 1 and phase 2. In this chapter, we have covered the health significances of the twenty core sirtfoods and why these foods have been recommended to be incorporated into your diet. As mentioned earlier, there are tons of other foods that may still be incorporated into your diet without retarding the effects of the sirtfoods. As we go on to describe specific recipes for breakfast, lunch, and dinner as you progress with your sirtfood diet, you would be noticing the other foods that can be incorporated into the sirtfood diet.

CHAPTER SIX
BREAKFAST RECIPES

I n this chapter, we would be examining the step-by-step process of creating amazing, mouth-watering sirtfood dishes that are perfect for breakfast. These foods have been carefully picked out to provide you with the energy and vigor you'd need to perform excellently all through your day while helping you to stay healthy, lose unhealthy fat, and look amazing. Let's dive right in!

1. SIRT MUESLI

Ingredients

- One-quarter cup of buckwheat flakes

- Two-thirds cup of buckwheat puffs

- Three tbsp. coconut flakes

- One-quarter cup Medjool dates

- One-eighth cup of chopped walnuts

- One and a half tbsp. of cocoa nibs

- Two-thirds cup of chopped strawberries

- 3/8 cup plain Greek Yoghurt

Preparation

- Simply mix all the ingredients in a clean bowl, and enjoy the fantastic goodness of this delicacy. However, only add strawberries and yogurt when you are ready to eat.

2. Sirtfood Omelet

Ingredients

- 2 oz. sliced bacon

- Three medium-sized eggs

- One and a one-quarter oz. sliced red endive

- 2 tbsp. chopped parsley

- One tsp. turmeric

- One tsp. extra virgin olive oil

Preparation

- Heat up a non-stick pan.

- Cut your bacon into thin strips.

- Cook your sliced bacon strips at high heat until they get crisp and crunchy. You do not have to add oil to the strips; the natural fat would help cook them.

- Remove the bacon strips from the pan once they're cooked, and place them on a paper towel to drain the extra fat.

- Wipe your pan clean and then pour in some oil – enough to cook the three eggs.

- Beat your eggs thoroughly and add in the turmeric, parsley, and endive.

- Chop your bacon into fine cubes and then stir the bits into the whisked eggs.

- Pour in oil into your pan and heat at medium heat.

- Pour the egg mixture in the hot oil and move the mixture around with a spatula

- Swirl the mixture carefully around the pan until the omelet is even.

- Lower the heat on your cooker and allow the omelet to firm up and even out at the edges.

- Fold your omelet in half, roll it up and serve hot.

3. Sirtfood Smoothie

Ingredients

- 3/8 cup of Greek yogurt

- Six walnut halves

- 10 hulled strawberries

- 7 – 10 kale leaves

- ¾ oz. dark chocolate

- One Medjool date

- ½ tsp. ground turmeric

- One sliver of Thai chili

- 200ml of unsweetened almond milk

Preparation

- Load up all the ingredients into your blender and grind into a smooth pulp.

4. YOGURT, BERRIES, WALNUTS, AND DARK CHOCOLATE.

This recipe is extremely simple and easy to follow and features the protein-packed Greek yogurt once again.

Ingredients

- One and twenty-five grams of mixed berries

- Two-thirds cup of plain Greek yogurt

- ¼ cup of walnuts

- 10g of dark chocolate (85% pure cocoa)

Preparation

- Get a clean bowl and add in your berries.

- Pour the plain Greek yogurt over the berries

- Add in your walnuts and dark chocolate, and food is ready.

5. SEASONED SCRAMBLED EGGS

This fantastic recipe allows you to relish the unbeatable taste and the amazing health benefits of scrambled eggs before you go to attack your day, fully loaded, and ready to go.

Ingredients

- One tsp. extra virgin olive oil

- 20g chopped red onions

- ½ chopped Thai chili

- 3 eggs (medium-sized)

- 50 ml of milk

- One tsp ground turmeric

- 2 tbsp. chopped parsley

Preparation

- Place a dry, non-stick frying pan on your cooker and set to medium heat.

- Fry your chili and red onions till they get soft without being browned.

- Whisk your eggs in a clean bowl and add in the milk, parsley, and turmeric.

- Pour the mixture into the hot pan and allow to cook at medium heat

- Move the egg mixture around in the pan to scramble it and prevent burning.

- Serve once desired consistency is achieved.

6. ASIAN SHRIMP STIR-FRY ALONG WITH BUCKWHEAT NOODLES

Ingredients

- Two teaspoons of deveined tamari sauce

- Seventy-five grams of buckwheat noodles

- One hundred and fifty grams of shelled raw jumbo shrimp

- Two pieces of garlic cloves

- One Thai chili (it should be finely chopped)

- One teaspoon of fresh ginger (finely chopped)

- Two teaspoons of extra virgin olive oil

- Twenty grams of red onions

- Forty-five grams of celery (sliced)

- Seventy-five grams of chopped green beans

- Fifty grams of chopped kale

- Half-a-cup of chicken stock

Preparation

- Get a frying pan (non-stick) and then use a high heat setting to heat it up.

- Proceed by frying the shrimp by using a single teaspoon of tamari sauce along with a single teaspoon of oil. Fry for four minutes.

- Have the shrimp transferred to a plate then use a clean paper towel to wipe the pan.

- In the hot water, cook the noodles for five to eight minutes, and strain.

- Proceed by frying the red onion, green beans, chili, ginger, garlic, kale and celery by using the leftover oil and tamari. Avoid including the celery leaves in that mixture. By using a medium heat setting, fry the ingredients for three-to-four minutes.

- Now include the stock to your mixture and allow it to cook till the vegs are done.

- The celery leaves, shrimp and noodles should now be added to the pan. Boil them. Once you're done, lower the heat then serve.

7. MISO AND SESAME GLAZED TOFU WITH GINGER AND CHILI STIR

Ingredients

- One tbsp mirin

- Twenty grams of miso paste

- One hundred and fifty grams of tofu

- Forty grams of celery

- Forty grams of red onion

- One hundred and twenty grams of zucchini

- One piece of Thai chili

- Two cloves of garlic

- One teaspoon of fresh ginger (finely chopped)

- Fifty grams of kale

- Two teaspoons of sesame seeds

- Thirty-five grams of buckwheat

- One teaspoon of ground turmeric

- Two teaspoons of extra virgin olive oil

- One teaspoon of tamari sauce

Preparation

- Heat your oven to four hundred degrees.

- Get a small roasting pan and line it with parchment paper.

- Combine the mirin and the miso.

- Slice up your tofu lengthwise, and then make each piece out into a triangular shape.

- Spread the miso mixture over the tofu and allow the tofu to get steeped in the mixture.

- Cut up your celery, red onion, and zucchini.

- Cut up the chili, garlic, and ginger.

- Allow the kale to gently cook in a steamer for five minutes.

- Transfer your tofu into the roasting pan and spread the sesame seeds over it. Allow the mixture to roast in the oven for twenty minutes.

- Rinse your buckwheat, and then sieve. Bring a pan filled with water to boil and add in the turmeric.

- Cook the buckwheat noodles and strain.

- Allow the oil to heat in a frying pan and then add the celery, onion, zucchini, chili, garlic, and ginger. Allow the entire mix to fry on high heat for two minutes. Reduce the heat to medium for four minutes until the vegetables are cooked.

- Add a tablespoon of water if the vegetables get stuck to the pan. Spread in the kale and tamari and allow the mixture to cook for another minute.

- Serve the cooked tofu with the greens and the buckwheat.

8. TURKEY ESCALOPE ALONG WITH SAGE, SPICED CAULIFLOWER, PARSLEY & CAPERS

Ingredients

- One hundred and fifty grams of chopped cauliflower

- Two garlic cloves

- Forty grams of red onions

- Two garlic cloves

- One Thai chili

- One teaspoon of chopped fresh ginger

- Two tablespoons of extra virgin olive oil

- Two teaspoons ground turmeric

- Thirty grams of sun-dried tomatoes

- Ten grams of fresh parsley

- One hundred and fifty grams of turkey steak

- One teaspoon of dried sage juice

- One-quarter lemon

- One tablespoon of capers

Preparation

- Put the raw cauliflower into your food processor.

- Chop up the cauliflower until a fine consistency is achieved.

- Fry the ginger, garlic, chili and red onions and ginger in the extra virgin olive oil until they are all reasonably soft.

- Put in your turmeric and cauliflower at this point, and allow the entire mixture to cook for one minute.

- Bring the mixture down form your cooker, then add the tomatoes and half of your parsley.

- Cover your turkey escalope with oil and sage and fry for six minutes, making sure to turn carefully to prevent burning.

- At this point, proceed by pouring in the lemon juice, parsley, capers, and one tablespoon of water to the pan to create your sauce.

9. BUCKWHEAT PANCAKES, MUSHROOMS, RED ONIONS, AND KALE SALAD

Ingredients

- One buckwheat pancake
- 50g button mushrooms
- Fifteen grams of chicken
- 200g Kale
- 20g red onions
- Extra Virgin Olive Oil

Preparation

- Clean and cut the button mushrooms.
- Clean and cut the kale into thin strips and the red onions into rings. Combine the green cabbage and

onion in a bowl, season with a drizzle of olive oil, and possibly a little lemon.

- Cut the chicken into pieces. In a pan, arrange a drizzle of olive oil and add the chicken pieces.

- Add the mushrooms and brown them.

- Place everything in the buckwheat pancake, and close the pancake.

- On a plate, arrange the green cabbage / red onion salad, then place the hot buckwheat pancake next to it. Enjoy your meal!

10. NAAN BREAD WITH BAKED TOFU AND CAULIFLOWER

Ingredients

- 50 g firm plain tofu

- 50 g cauliflower

- ½ clove garlic

- ½ small onion

- 50ml of water

- 50ml coconut milk

- ½ tablespoon of tomato puree

- ½ teaspoon powdered Indian broth

- ½ tablespoon coconut oil

- ½ teaspoon curry powder

- ½ teaspoon cumin

- ½ tablespoon potato starch

Naan bread:

- 75g wheat flour

- One plain yogurt

- Two pinches of sugar

- 5g baker's yeast or 8 g dehydrated yeast

- 5g salt

- Two tablespoons extra virgin olive oil

- 5 cl lukewarm water

- One teaspoon caraway seeds

Preparation

- Peel and mince the garlic and the onions.

- In a casserole dish, sauté everything in coconut oil

with the curry and cumin until lightly colored.

- Add the coconut milk, the tomato puree, and 50 ml of water and the Indian broth. Mix well then bring to a dainty simmer.

- Add the tofu pieces and the cauliflower.

- Cook gently without the lid on for about 20 min until the cauliflower is slightly tender.

- Dilute the starch with a little cooking juice, then pour back into the casserole dish and continue cooking for 5 min.

- Serve with basmati rice and naan bread.

Naan Bread

- Put the flour in your food processor.

- Add the crumbled yeast, olive oil, sugar, yogurt, caraway seeds, and mix well.

- Proceed by adding the water and continue mixing with the whisk until the dough is soft and comes off the sides of your bowl.

- Now place the ball of dough in a small bowl then cover, and allow to stand for thirty minutes.

- Heat up an empty pan, and cook the naan bread on each side for four minutes to remove moisture.

- Enjoy your mouth-watering delicacy.

CHAPTER SEVEN
SUGGESTED LUNCH RECIPES

I n this chapter, we would be reviewing in detail the ingredients and steps needed to prepare some of the most delicious and healthy sirtfoods suitable for lunch.

1. SALMON FILLET, ENDIVE, ARUGULA AND CELERY

Ingredients

- 200g fresh salmon fillet

- 200g arugula

- Three red endives

- One large pink grapefruit

- Two slices of smoked salmon

- One small shallot

- One lemon

- Grated Parmesan cheese

- Extra virgin olive oil

- One teaspoon balsamic vinegar

- Salt and pepper to taste

Preparation

- Cut the lemon in half to gently extract the liquid juice inside it.

- Peel the grapefruit over a bowl to collect the juice. Detach the quarters and cut them into pieces.

- Peel and chop the shallot.

- Remove the skin and bones from the fresh salmon fillet, then dice into small pieces

- Place the whole mixture in a salad bowl, sprinkle with the lime and grapefruit juice, mix and let stand aside.

- Cut the bottoms of the endives, remove the damaged leaves, and chop the main parts into thin strips.

- Wash and wring the arugula.

- Carefully cut the smoked salmon slices into light strips.

- Drain the marinated salmon fillet well, and keep two teaspoons of the marinade.

- Emulsify the marinade with olive oil and balsamic vinegar in a bowl, then salt and pepper as desired.

- In a salad bowl, mix the diced salmon fillet, the smoked salmon strips, the pieces of grapefruit, the arugula, the minced endives, and the olive oil sauce. Turn to mix and sprinkle lightly with grated Parmesan cheese.

- Serve this salad immediately and serve with slices of toast. Do not hesitate to double the proportions if you want to enjoy it as a main dish.

2. TUSCAN BEAN STEW

Ingredients

- Two teaspoons extra virgin olive oil

- 6 oz. cooked chicken sausages cut lengthwise in half

and sliced

- 10 oz. fresh mushrooms

- One small raw red onion

- Two thinly sliced garlic cloves

- 29 oz. canned, diced tomatoes

- Sixteen oz. canned beans

- One medium uncooked zucchini

- One tbsp. rosemary

- ¼ tsp salt

- 2 oz. arugula

- ¼ cups Grated Parmesan Cheese

Preparation

- By using a Dutch oven, set the heat level to medium-high.

- Add the sausages and cook, often stirring, until lightly browned, about three minutes.

- Using a cooking spoon, transfer to a small bowl or plate.

- Add the mushrooms and onion to the pot and cook, often stirring, until the vegetables are tender, usually for about three minutes.

- Now add the garlic and cook, constantly stirring for about 30 seconds.

- Add the sausages to the tomatoes, beans, zucchini, rosemary, and salt and allow to boil.

- Lower the heat and simmer, till the mushrooms becomes soft, usually after about 2 minutes.

- Remove from heat and stir in the arugula until it is softened.

- Pour the stew into four bowls and garnish evenly with Parmesan.

3. STRAWBERRY BUCKWHEAT SALAD

Ingredients
Tamari dressing:

- One-quarter cup of olive oil

- Two tablespoons of vinegar

- One tablespoon of reduced salt tamari sauce

- One tablespoon of old-fashioned mustard

Salad:

- One cup buckwheat, rinsed and drained

- 6 cups mixed lettuce

- 2 cups strawberries, hulled and sliced

- A half fennel bulb cut into thin slices

- One-third cup of red onion, cut into thin strips

- Six cooked bacon slices, chopped

- One-third cup of roasted sunflower seeds

- Salt and pepper

Preparation
Tamari vinaigrette

- In a small jar, put the olive oil, rice vinegar, tamari sauce, and old-fashioned mustard. Add in some pepper.

- Close the lid and shake vigorously.

Salad preparation

- Now place the buckwheat in a medium-sized bowl and cover with at least 2 inches (5 cm) of water. Cover the bowl and let soak in the refrigerator overnight. Drain buckwheat, rinse with cold water, and drain again.

- In a large bowl, put the lettuce, strawberries, fennel, onion, bacon, sunflower seeds, and reserved buckwheat. Add in your dressing and mix well.

4. SAUTÉED POTATOES IN CHICKEN BROTH

Ingredients

- Six medium-sized potatoes

- One onion

- Chicken broth

- 100ml of water

- One tbsp extra virgin olive oil

- Salt to taste

Preparation

- First peel the potatoes then slice it across into pieces.

- Proceed by peeling the onions and chop into small pieces.

- Fry minced onion pieces in oil for five minutes. Add in the potatoes and cook for another ten minutes while stirring gently.

- Dilute the chicken broth with water and add to the cooker, and cook for five minutes.

- Add salt to taste and serve.

5. BAKED POTATOES AND CHILI CON CARNE

Ingredients

- 8Big potatoes

- 600g Knife ground beef

- 35cl Beef broth

- 500g Crushed tomatoes

- 500g Canned kidney beans

- 1 tbsp. Tomato puree

- 2 Big onions

- One bunch of chives

- Two garlic cloves

- Half teaspoon Chili powder

- One tbsp. Cumin

- One tbsp. dried oregano

- 2 tbsp. Extra Virgin Olive Oil

- 250g Farm fresh cream

- Salt and pepper to taste

Preparation

- Peel and chop the onions and garlic.

- Heat the broth in a saucepan.

- Heat the oil available in the frying pan to fry the onions and garlic for five minutes while mixing.

- Add the meat and allow to cook for five minutes over high heat. Add salt and pepper.

- Pour the tomatoes and the tomato puree, then the broth.

- Add the cumin, oregano, and chili, and then mix. Cover and simmer 45 minutes.

- Add the beans, cover, and continue cooking over low heat, 20 min.

- Preheat the oven to 180 ° C

- Wash the potatoes. Once done, wrap them together in aluminum foil and bake for 30 to 35 minutes.

- Remove the paper, cut the potatoes in half and scoop it out slightly to garnish with chili.

- Top each potato with a spoonful of cream

- Serve hot.

6. CHICKEN IN PEPPER SAUCE

Ingredients

- One jar of 340 ml roasted peppers

- One cup (250 mL) canned coconut milk

- Fifteen ml red wine vinegar

- Two cloves of garlic

- One tsp. paprika

- One tsp. dried oregano

- One tsp. salt

- One-quarter cup of chopped fresh parsley, chopped

- One tbsp extra virgin olive oil

- Four boneless skinless chicken breasts or thighs

- Salt and pepper

- One minced onion

- One red bell pepper (minced)

- One-quarter cup of chopped fresh parsley, for garnish

Preparation

- In a blender, mix all the ingredients for the sauce (everything above except chicken, olive oil, onions, salt, and pepper) until you get a mixture of smooth consistency.

- Place a rack at the center of your oven and preheat to 400 ° F.

- In your large non-stick skillet (you can use a cast iron), heat the olive oil over high heat and fry the chicken breasts. Generously season with salt and pepper. Give it time by allowing all the sides of the chicken to fry for at least three minutes and then set aside on a plate.

- Lower the heat level back to medium then add the onions, and allow to heat for six minutes over medium heat, stirring often.

- Add the red pepper and cook for another minute only.

- Return the chicken to the pan and sprinkle with the roasted pepper sauce.

- Bake the dish for fifteen minutes. Before serving, remove from the oven and grace it by adding some parsley. Serve with pasta in olive oil and chives or white rice.

7. WALDORF SALAD

Ingredients

- One hundred and twenty-five grams of mayonnaise

- Two tablespoons white vinegar

- One apple, peeled and cut into pieces

- One celery stalk, diced

- One hundred and twenty-five grams of grapes

- One hundred and twenty-five grams of chopped

walnuts

- Salt and pepper to taste

Preparation

- In a large bowl, whisk the mayonnaise and vinegar.

- Add the apple, celery, raisins, and walnuts.

- Sprinkle in salt and pepper. Mix everything and serve fresh.

8. WHOLE WHEAT PITA

Ingredients:

- 250g of whole wheat flour

- 2 tbsp extra virgin olive oil

- 5g salt

- 10g dry baker's yeast

- One hundred and fifty-ml hot water

Preparation

- Add the whole flour and the salt in a bowl and stir. Then add the rest of the ingredients: oil, yeast, and water. Stir thoroughly to mix.

- Mix all the ingredients well until the pita bread dough is formed. Knead the dough for a few minutes on the table. If the dough seem to be too dry, you can add a little more water.

- Once kneaded, make the dough into a ball and put it in a bowl. Have it covered and let it be there for two hours.

- Take out the whole pita bread dough and knead again. Work the dough into balls of about 80g each. Use a roller to make the dough well-rounded. Make the pieces of bread ten-to-twelve cm wide and One cm thick.

- Put the pitas on a tray. Preheat the oven to 200 ° C, slot in the tray, and let the pieces of bread bake for ten minutes, depending on the oven.

- Finally, take out the pieces of bread, let them cool a little and serve!

9. SCRAMBLED TOFU WITH MUSHROOMS (VEGAN)

Ingredients

- One hundred and twenty-five grams of plain firm tofu

- 100g silky tofu

- One tbsp. fresh cream

- One tbsp. sesame puree

- One tsp. Mustard

- ½ tsp. ground turmeric

- Four sprigs of fresh chives

- Half onion (optional)

- One garlic clove (optional)

- 50g mushrooms

- 2 tbsp. Extra Virgin Olive Oil

- One tbsp. Tamari soy sauce (gluten-free, organic soy sauce)

- Salt and pepper to taste

Preparation

- In a bowl, crush the firm tofu, add in the silky tofu, cream, tahini, mustard, turmeric, and chopped chives.

- Mix thoroughly, and add salt and pepper to taste.

- Peel and chop the onion and the garlic.

- Rinse the mushrooms under a stream of water. Cut off the ends of the stalks and cut the mushrooms into strips. Gently fry the mushrooms, onions, and garlic over medium-high heat in a pan with a little olive oil.

- Once the mushrooms, onions, and garlic are very tender and slightly brown in color, add the mixture to the tofu and cook over medium heat for about 5 minutes. Stir the mixture continuously with a spatula.

- Serve hot, and enjoy.

10. PASTA WITH SMOKED SALMON AND ARUGULA

Ingredients

- 250g Spaghetti

- One hundred and fifty grams of Smoked salmon

- One bunch of arugula

- 2 tbsp. Extra virgin olive oil

- One finely chopped onion

- Salt and pepper to taste

Preparation

- Cook the pasta in boiling water for ten minutes. Add salt to taste.

- Slice the smoked salmon into strips. Rinse and wring the arugula.

- Heat One tablespoonful of extra virgin olive oil in a frying pan and chop the onion. Add in the drained spaghetti, the salmon strips, and the arugula. Mix well and cook for 2 min.

- Sprinkle in the rest of the olive oil, salt, and pepper.

- Mix and serve hot.

CHAPTER EIGHT
SUGGESTED DINNER RECIPES

In this chapter, we would be reviewing ten amazing sirtfood recipes that can ideally be made for dinner.

1. FUSILLI SALAD WITH BUCKWHEAT, PESTO, TOMATOES, AND PINE NUTS

Ingredients

- 200g buckwheat fusilli

- Sixteen cherry tomatoes

- 80g dried tomatoes

- 40g pine nuts

- Salt and pepper

- 4 tbsp. basil pesto

Basil Pesto:

- One bunch of basil

- 2 tbsp. olive oil

- 50g parmesan

- 60g pine nuts

- One clove of garlic all mixed

Preparation

- Cook the pasta for ten minutes, add salt to taste. Drain and let it cool.

- Cut the cherry tomatoes in half, chop the dried tomatoes into thin strips and lightly toast the pine nuts in a pan for one minute.

- In a large bowl, gently mix the pasta and pesto. Add the dried tomatoes, half of the chopped basil and the pine nuts. Carefully stir the entire mixture and add seasoning to taste.

- Arrange the cherry tomatoes and the rest of the chopped basil on the salad.

2. TOFU AND MUSHROOM SOUP

Ingredients

- 500ml vegetable broth (or 500 ml of water and One tbsp. dehydrated vegetable broth)

- 375ml Soy beverage

- 250g button mushrooms ready to use

- 240g herb tofu

- 4 tbsp. tapioca

- One medium onion

- One tbsp. canola oil

- One tbsp. parsley

- Pepper to taste

Preparation

- Rinse the mushrooms thoroughly and cut them into pieces.

- Peel the onion and dice it.

- Heat the oil over medium heat in a saucepan. Sauté the onion in the oil for one minute, and then add the mushrooms and cook for five minutes, stirring occasionally.

- While the mushrooms and onion cook cut the diced tofu, and wash and chop your parsley.

- Add the vegetable broth and soy beverage to the mixture cooking.

- Add the tapioca into the mixture, then add the tofu. Continue cooking over low heat for about seven minutes.

- Sprinkle with chopped parsley and serve.

3. SALMON SALAD AND FRESH MINT

Ingredients

- Salad leaves

- 200 g of fresh salmon

- Six mint leaves

- Thrcc tablespoons of white cheese

- Two limes

- Salad dressing

- Onc large cucumber

Preparation

- Peel the cucumber and remove the seeds. Cut the cucumber into thin rings and put it in a colander.

- Steam your salmon for 8 minutes. Mash the salmon in a bowl and mix in the cottage cheese with the lemon, salt, and pepper

- Add the chopped mint, mix well, and refrigerate.

- Place the salad in strips on a plate and add in the cucumber salmon and enjoy!

4. GRANOLA WITH HAZELNUTS AND CHOCOLATE CHIPS

Ingredients

- Four small oatmeal packs

- 2 tbsp. coconut oil

- Two whole hazelnut packs

- One 200 bar of dark chocolate

- 4 tbsp maple syrup

Preparation:

- Preheat your oven to 150°C

- Cut your hazelnuts and chocolate bar into small

pieces.

- In a medium-sized bowl, mix the oats, coconut oil, hazelnut chips, and the maple syrup to give a paste.

- Spread the paste over a sheet of baking paper. Keep the thickness at half a centimeter at most.

- Bake halfway and cook for about thirty minutes until the mixture is slightly brown.

- Take the baking sheet out of the oven and, using a zester or a cheese grater, grind the whole four squares of chocolate you have kept whole. Make it right out of the oven when the dough is still hot.

- Allow to cool and mix your granola with the chocolate chips.

5. CHICKEN TAGINE WITH SQUASH AND MEDJOOL DATES

Ingredients

- One large chicken cut into eight pieces

- 4 tbsp. extra virgin olive oil

- 2 tbsp flaked almonds

- Two chopped onions

- One.5 tsp ground cumin

- One tsp coriander seeds

- One tbsp. ground cinnamon

- Two garlic cloves (chopped)

- Two slices of fresh ginger

- One sachet of saffron

- Salt and pepper to taste

- 500 ml chicken broth

- 750g peeled squash

- Six large pitted dates cut in half

- One bunch of fresh coriander

- Orange zest

Preparation

- Leniently toast the almonds in your frying pan and set aside.

- Proceed by heating a little fraction of oil in a Dutch oven and fry the onions for about five-to-six minutes, continue stirring until they are slightly brown.

- Add in the cumin, previously crushed coriander seeds, cinnamon, and garlic. Now cook for roughly two minutes then add the chicken, ginger and saffron, salt, and pepper.

- Cover the entire mixture with chicken broth and bake in a covered oven for One hour.

- Add the squash, dates, and orange zest. Continue cooking for about 20-25 minutes.

- Remove the ginger and serve on a bed of couscous. Add in the cooking broth and garnish with chopped fresh coriander and toasted almonds.

6. SHRIMP AND ARRABBIATA SAUCE

Ingredients

- One onion, chopped

- One tsp crushed hot pepper flakes

- 5 tbsp. Extra Virgin Olive Oil

- Two garlic cloves, chopped

- 60 ml white wine

- 28 oz. crushed Italian tomatoes

- 375g pasta

- 454g large raw shrimp (peeled)

- 2 tbsp Chopped parsley

- One cup grated Parmesan Cheese

- Salt and pepper

Preparation

- Get a saucepan then add the three tablespoons of oil, sauté the onion and the pepper in the oil then heat. You should also add some pepper and salt to taste.

- Add the garlic and continue cooking for One minute. Deglaze with white wine.

- Add the tomatoes and continue cooking for about ten minutes.

- Boil your pasta. Add in a little salt and oil. Drain and serve.

- In a large skillet heated over high heat, heat the shrimp in hot oil. Add salt and pepper to taste.

- Add the sauce and allow the mixture to boil.

- Add the pasta and parsley and season to taste.

- Serve warm. You can also shower it with Parmesan cheese if desired.

7. TURMERIC SALMON AND COCONUT MILK

Ingredients

- Two skinless salmon steaks

- One onion

- One garlic clove

- One tsp. turmeric

- 10 cl coconut milk

- 10 cl of fish stock

- 4 tbsp. Extra Virgin Olive oil

- Salt and pepper to taste

Preparation

- Peel and chop the onion and garlic. Fry on low heat for 3 minutes in a saucepan with two tablespoons of olive oil.

- Add the turmeric, cook for 30 seconds, and then pour the coconut milk and the fish stock.

- Add in pepper and salt to taste and cook over very low heat for 10 minutes.

- Cook the salmon steaks over high heat in a pan with two tablespoons of olive oil. Cook each side for One to 2 minutes.

- Serve the fish with the sauce.

8. CORONATION CHICKEN SALAD WITH CHEESE

Ingredients

- 200g chicken cutlet

- One hundred and seventy-five grams of spelled flour

- 75g cottage cheese

- 50g ground almonds

- Three eggs

- One onion

- Half tsp. baking powder

- 2 tbsp. Extra Virgin Olive Oil

- 10 cl whole milk

- One tbsp. pepper

- One tsp. nutmeg

Preparation

- Warm by using the extra virgin olive oil in a non-stick pan, add the minced onions and the diced chicken and allow the mixture to fry until slightly brown.

- Melt the cheese in a bowl, add the eggs, flour, yeast, oil, and warm milk.

- Add the mixture to the chicken. Sprinkle in the pepper, nutmeg, and finally, the powdered almonds.

- Mix well, then pour the dough into a mold and bake for about 40 minutes in an oven preheated to One80 ° C.

- Serve warm with a salad.

9. BAKED POTATOES AND CHICKPEA STEW

Ingredients

- 4-6 baking potatoes

- One tbsp. canola oil

- One tbsp. cumin seeds

- One red onion (finely chopped)

- Five garlic cloves (minced)

- One tbsp. ground coriander seeds

- One can of chickpeas (drained)

- One cup of water

- One red potato (diced)

- 2 tsp. chopped fresh cilantro

- Half tsp. salt

- Half tsp. coarsely ground pepper

- One tomato (diced)

Preparation

- Preheat your oven to 200°C, and add in your baking potatoes for an hour.

- By using a medium-high heat settings for the saucepan, heat the oil in it to fry the cumin seeds for 10 seconds till they are slightly brown, then add the onion and garlic and stir till they are slightly brown too. Finally, add the coriander and stir for another thirty seconds.

- Add the chickpeas, water, potato, and one tsp. of fresh cilantro. Add in salt and pepper to taste.

- Lower the heat and boil the entire mixture. Cover then simmer for fifteen minutes till the potato is soft.

- Proceed by adding the diced tomatoes then increase the heat slightly. Allow cooking for One-to-two minutes.

- Garnish with the leftover fresh cilantro and serve with the baked potatoes.

10. CHICKEN SALAD WITH SESAME SEEDS

Ingredients

- Two chicken strips

- Mixed salad (Californian style)

- One onion (finely chopped)

- One tbsp. sesame seeds

- One tsp. Almonds

- One tbsp. Dijon's mustard

- 2 tbsp. Extra Virgin Olive oil

- One tbsp. Balsamic vinegar

- One Lemon

- Bacon (to taste)

Preparation

- Warm by using the extra virgin olive oil in a non-stick pan over high heat.

- Fry the chicken breasts in the pan with a little mustard to add flavor.

- Prepare the vinaigrette with oil, balsamic vinegar, finely chopped onions, and a little mustard. Stir the mixture thoroughly and leave to marinate.

- Wash and cut the salad leaves, and then mix the salad and the vinaigrette.

- Cut the chicken strips into thin slices.

- Peel the bacon and place everything on the salad.

- Sprinkle in the almonds and sesame seeds. Add fresh lemon zest to taste.

CHAPTER NINE
SIRTFOOD SNACKS AND DESSERTS

It is imminent that at some points during your day, you would feel a pang hunger and have the urge to grab a snack. If you are the kind of person that used to eat a lot of junk foods before, the healthy snacks and desserts classified as sirtfood bites can help you to prevent relapsing into eating unhealthy foods, as they are portable, fill you up temporarily and are delectably tasty. In this chapter, we would be reviewing ten sirtfood snacks and desserts.

1. GREEN TEA

Ingredients

- Onc tbsp. green tea powder

- One cup of water

Preparation

- Simply dissolve the green tea powder in the glass of water and enjoy it.

2. RED GRAPES

Ingredients

- 5 – 10 pieces of red grapes

Preparation

- Simply rinse the grapes under running water and enjoy.

3. APPLES

Ingredients

- 2 -3 Apples

Preparation

- Simply rinse your Apples under running water and enjoy

4. DARK CHOCOLATE

Ingredients

- One bar of 85% dark cocoa chocolate

Preparation

- Remove the dark chocolate from its wrapping and slowly savor with water or green tea.

5. COCOA

Ingredients

- Two tsp. of pure cocoa powder

- One cup of water

- 30ml milk

- One tsp. sugar

Preparation

- Pour in the cocoa, milk, and sugar into the glass.

- In your kettle, warm the water inside it, or get some water out of your refrigerator.

- Mix the water and the mixture in the cup, and enjoy it.

6. OLIVES

Ingredients

- Six large black or green olives

Preparation

- Simply rinse the olives under running water, and serve at room temperature.

7. BLACKBERRIES

Ingredients

- Ten-to-fifteen blackberries

Preparation

- For optimum satisfaction, keep your blackberries refrigerated for four to five hours, and enjoy chilled.

8. POMEGRANATE SEEDS

Ingredients

- 50g pomegranate seeds

Preparation

- Unleash the goodness of this healthy sirtfood snack by simply popping half of a pack in your mouth when you feel hungry in the middle of the day, or after a meal.

9. BLUEBERRIES

Ingredients

- 25 pieces of blueberries

Preparation

- Simply rinse your berries under running water, or retrieve from your refrigerator after four to five hours, and enjoy.

10.   STRAWBERRIES

Ingredients

- 50g of strawberries

Preparation

- Keep the strawberries refrigerated for a few hours, and enjoy as a fruity snack or dessert.

CHAPTER TEN
21-DAYS MEAL PLAN

Experts in psychology have proven repeatedly over the years that it takes 21 days for the average human being to build a habit, and 90 days for that habit to become fully incorporated into his lifestyle. Building a habit can be challenging if you do not have a solid game plan, and that is our ambition for this chapter. In this chapter, we would build a 21-days sirtfood timetable that would help you get through Phases One and Two of the Sirtfood diet. Let's get moving!

PHASE ONE

DAY 1:

Breakfast: Sirtfood Green Juice

Lunch: Sirt Muesli

Dinner: Sirtfood Green Juice

DAY 2:

Breakfast: Sirtfood Green Juice

Lunch: Spicy scrambled eggs

Dinner: Sirtfood Green Juice

DAY 3:

Breakfast: Sirtfood Green Juice

Lunch: Buckwheat Pasta Salad

Dinner: Sirtfood Green Juice

DAY 4:

Breakfast: Mushroom and Tofu Scramble

Lunch: Sirtfood smoothie

Dinner: Sirtfood Green Juice

DAY 5:

Breakfast: Sirt Tuna Salad

Lunch: Pasta with Smoked Salmon and Arugula

Dinner: Sirtfood Green Juice

DAY 6:

Breakfast: Sirtfood Omelet

Lunch: Salmon Fillet, Endive, Arugula, and Celery

Dinner: Sirtfood Green Juice

DAY 7:

Breakfast: Yoghurt, Berries, Dark Chocolate & Walnuts

Lunch: Tuscan Bean Stew

Dinner: Sirtfood Green Juice

PHASE TWO

DAY 8:

Breakfast: Seasoned Scrambled Eggs

Lunch: Strawberry Buckwheat Salad

Dinner: Fusilli Salad with Buckwheat, Tomatoes, Pesto and Pine nuts

DAY 9:

Breakfast: The Common Asian Shrimp Stir-Fry along with Buckwheat Noodles

Lunch: Sautéed Potatoes in Chicken Broth

Dinner: Tofu and Mushroom Soup

DAY 10:

Breakfast: The miso & Sesame Glazed Tofu along with Ginger & Chili Stir

Lunch: Baked Potatoes and Chili Con Carne

Dinner: Salmon Salad and Fresh Mint

DAY 11:

Breakfast: Sage along with Turkey Escalope, Spiced Cauliflower, Parsley and Capers

Lunch: Chicken in Pepper Sauce

Dinner: Granola with Hazelnuts and Chocolate Chips

DAY 12:

Breakfast: Buckwheat Pancakes, Mushrooms, Red Onions & Kale Salad

Lunch: Waldorf Salad

Dinner: Chicken Tagine with Squash and Medjool Dates

DAY 13:

Breakfast: Naan Bread with Baked Tofu and Cauliflower

Lunch: Whole Wheat Pita

Dinner: Shrimp and Arrabbiata Sauce

DAY 14:

Breakfast: Sirt Muesli

Lunch: Scrambled Tofu with Mushrooms

Dinner: Turmeric Salmon and Coconut Milk

DAY 15:

Breakfast: Sirtfood Omelet

Lunch: Pasta with Smoked Salmon and Arugula

Dinner: Coronation Chicken Salad with Cheese

DAY 16:

Breakfast: Sirtfood smoothie

Lunch: Salmon Fillet, Arugula, Endive, and Celery

Dinner: Baked Potatoes and Chickpea Stew

DAY 17:

Breakfast: Yogurt, Berries, Dark Chocolate & Walnuts

Lunch: Tuscan Bean Stew

Dinner: Chicken Salad with Sesame Seeds

DAY 18:

Breakfast: Seasoned Scrambled Eggs

Lunch: Strawberry Buckwheat Salad

Dinner: Tofu and Mushroom Soup

DAY 19:

Breakfast: Asian Shrimp Stir-Fry with Buckwheat Noodles

Lunch: Sautéed Potatoes in Chicken Broth

Dinner: Salmon Salad and Fresh Mint

DAY 20:

Breakfast: Miso and Sesame Glazed Tofu with Ginger and Chili Stir

Lunch: Baked Potatoes and Chili Con Carne

Dinner: Granola with Hazelnuts and Chocolate Chips

DAY 21:

Breakfast: Turkey Escalope along with Sage, Spiced Cauliflower, Parsley & Capers

Lunch: Chicken in Pepper Sauce

Dinner: Chicken Tagine with Squash and Medjool Dates

CHAPTER ELEVEN
TROUBLESHOOTING AND
FREQUENTLY ASKED QUESTIONS

L ife is rarely ever a bed of roses, and most times, before significant victories are recorded, intense sacrifices need to be made. The sirtfood diet may seem simple and easily practicable on paper; however, when it comes to the actual execution, a couple of common problems seems to rear their heads. In this chapter, we would be examining some of the common problems that most individuals face during the course of the diet and how these challenges can be handled in the long run. We would also be answering some of the most frequently asked questions about the sirtfood diet.

Troubleshooting

1. The Problem of Cravings

In today's 'sweet' modern world, a lot of people are severely hooked on junk food and sugary snacks, and this addiction poses one of the strongest problems against progress in the sirtfood diet. Weight loss and heavy consumption of processed sugar just don't go together. As has been reiterated in the past chapters, when you consume a lot of processed sugar, your blood sugar levels rise accordingly, leading to a corresponding rise in your insulin levels. Elevated insulin levels lead to accumulated fat deposits. If you really desire the trim body, fitness, agility, and mental alertness that comes with staying steadfast through the sirtfood diet, then you must break your bad habit of compulsively consuming processed sugar.

One proven way to help you break your unhealthy addiction to sugar is to keep busy. Irrespective of where you're; home or school, be sure to keep yourself gainfully occupied doing something. Planning out your day right from the start can help to prevent situations where you end up unnecessarily idle and start considering getting a cake or an ice cream. Stay busy, productive, and focus, and your cravings will take a nosedive.

Drinking your sirtfood juice constantly throughout the first phase of the sirtfood diet and afterward would also help you keep your cravings at bay. The sirtfood green juice is packed with a variety of leafy greens that supply your body with essential nutrients and vitamins that keep you invigorated. The sirtfood juice does not only help you stay healthy; it provides you with an alternative you can turn to when the cravings come calling. To help you resist the urge to indulge in your sugary treats, you can also take advantage of the sirtfood bites described earlier in this book. Packing a box of blueberries or a bar of dark chocolate in your backpack of handbag can help provide you with something healthy to munch on as you work to prevent your cravings from overwhelming you.

Your mind will be your most powerful asset as you embark on the sirtfood diet. You need to imbibe self-discipline and constantly remind yourself of why you started this journey in the first place. Never forget that success in life is all about sacrifices, and the sacrifice you would have to make for long-term well-being is letting go of the sweet but deadly things holding you back. The realization that the desperate cravings would die down soon is also one that you need to keep at the back of your mind as you go through every single day of your sirtfood diet.

Finally, to help you win this war against your cravings, try as much as possible to distance yourself from your triggers. If you have a stash of cupcakes, muffins, or ice cream in your refrigerator, it may be time to give those foods out. Inform your friends about your new diet, so theta they can encourage you when your resolve goes weak, and so that they can control their consumption of sugary treats around you. As much as possible, it is advisable for you to avoid places like pastry shops and ice cream shacks in the early days of your diet so that you do not falter.

2. The Problem of Hunger

Hunger is another extremely common obstacle to success in the sirtfood diet, especially in phase One, where stringent calorie restrictions exist. To help you deal with the problem of hunger, try to deal with less physically exerting activities as your body gets used to surviving on lower calories. Don't push your body to the limits at this time. Keep your exercise light and rest as much as possible. Keeping your sirtfood juice handy also helps you to refuel from time to time, and helps to curb the hunger and exhaustion. Closely related to the problem of hunger during the first few days of the diet is the issue of fatigue and exhaustion. When hunger comes around, tiredness and inactivity almost automatically follow. So to help you stay strong in your first few days of this diet, rest as much as possible, avoid extreme physical exertion, and of course, don't forget to drink your sirtfood juice.

3. The Problem of Relapsing

A lot of people go into diets with one single aim: Not to relapse. It is good to keep it in mind that you have to inculcate the self-discipline needed to pull off the rigorous sirtfood diet. However, your main aim should be to last as long as possible and eventually integrate the sirtfood diet into your lifestyle. People make mistakes and slip once or twice sometimes. Forgive yourself, pick yourself back up, and keep moving. Note that this is not a license for you to go ahead and start sneaking ice cream into your mouth on the third day of your diet. This is simply to let you realize that if you make a mistake, that doesn't mean your diet is over. Pick yourself back up, remove as much of the negative triggers as possible from your environment, and be determined to achieve your long-term health goals.

4. Being Unsure of What to Eat

The sirtfood diet contains a wonderfully wide variety of healthy foods. We understand that picking out exactly what to eat on one particular day might be quite challenging since you might be new to most of the foods on the list. This is why we have designed the 2One-day meal plan in the previous chapter for you to refer to. If you have a designed meal plan available, you don't need to stress yourself out trying to decide what to eat. Simply consult your guide and get cooking.

5. Being Too Busy to Cook

Factualism has it clear that we live in a very fast-paced world where a lot of people have to battle with insane deadlines and mind-numbing workloads. We understand that finding the time to cook three times a day under these conditions may be difficult. So, we recommend that you cook some of your meals in advance, keep them in your refrigerator, and simply get microwave them if necessary before eating. For those early mornings when you need to quickly dash out, you can choose some of the simpler recipes such as the Sirt Muesli, the Sirtfood Smoothie, the Sirtfood Omelet, the spicy scrambled eggs, and other simpler options that require minimal preparation time and efforts. Success in any endeavor in the modern world is all about flexibility, and the sirtfood diet provides you with a lot of that.

6. The Temptation to Eat Out

It is a comprehensible fact that you would miss your old

diners and restaurants as you begin to settle into your sirtfood diet routine. Perhaps, you even used to go out with your friends to have dinner at a specific restaurant. Once your first two phases are over, you can eat out, but ensure to eat plant-rich dishes, avoid bread and fried foods, eat slowly, and be sure to stop when you are full. Once again, having a reliable support system comes in handy in this situation. Let your friends understand that you are going through a particularly tasking diet, and you would like them to help you stay steadfast in your goals.

7. The Problem of Over-eating

As humans, our appetites differ from one person to another. However, eating too much wouldn't do you too much good in the long run. It is not compulsory for you to finish your entire plate of food. Once you are 80% full, let the remaining food go. Don't allow guilt to overwhelm you and force you back down a road of obesity and unhealthiness. Also, watch your pace of eating. If you're always in haste when eating, you are likely to over-eat. So, eat slowly instead, and note your level of satiety. Once you feel full and energized, stop. This will help you curb the problem of eating too much and overloading your body with calories.

8. Alcohol Addiction

If you are excessively addicted to alcohol, then successfully integrating the sirtfood diet into your lifestyle and reaping its amazing benefits may be extremely challenging. For a start, try to focus your time and energy on other productive activities. When the urge to drink hits, find something else – something productive and engaging – to do. Being associated to support group such as the Alcoholics Anonymous groups may also help you gradually let go of this bad habit. Keeping your friends in the loop about your decision to quit drinking will also go a long way in helping to keep your cravings for alcohol in check. Avoid pubs and bars as much as possible, and if the problem persists, then you might need to take to a medical expert about what to do to eradicate your addiction to alcohol.

Other Frequently Asked Questions
9. Should I exercise while on the Sirtfood diet?

Yes, of course! Light workouts increase the efficiency of the sirtfood diet and help you progress faster on your journey to losing weight, achieving enhanced mental clarity, and reducing the risk of long-term chronic diseases. So, keep your workouts simple, limit physical exertion, but try as much as possible to exercise every single day.

10.   Can the Sirtfood Diet rectify extreme obesity?

A lot of people believe that diets only work for overweight people, and full-blown obesity can only be corrected by surgical procedures. The decision of whether you need surgery to remove the excess fat deposits would depend on your doctor. However, if your cardiac health is not in immediate danger, the sirtfood diet can help you to make immense progress in the long-run by helping you to consistently shed your fat deposits while consolidating on your muscle mass gains.

11. Should I continue with the Sirtfood Diet after hitting my Target Weight?

The aim of the sirtfood diet is to help you to build a healthy routine that would allow you to stay healthy and disease-free in the long term. Even after reaching your target weight, try as much as possible to keep sirtfoods dominant in your diet, and avoid forbidden foods such as alcohol and processed sugar as much as possible. Sticking to the basic rules will help prevent you from gaining excess weight again. Remember to also keep exercising and going for regular medical check-ups if necessary.

12. How many times should I drink the Sirtfood Green Juice per day?

This is quite a common question among people who are just getting familiar with the sirtfood diet. Because of the intense calorie restriction in the first three days of phase one, it is recommended that you consume three cups of the sirtfood green juice per day for those three days. For the subsequent four days of Phase One, the sirtfood juice can be consumed twice per day. From phase 2 onwards, it is okay to keep the consumption of the juice at one cup per day; to be taken before breakfast in the morning to help give you your daily dose of green vitality.

13. Can I embark on the Sirtfood Diet if I'm on special medication?

If you are using meds, then you might need to talk to your doctor before starting the diet. However, even if your meds wouldn't allow you to go through the intense calorie restrictions of phase one, you can still incorporate sirtfoods into your diet and enjoy the amazing goodness that comes from consuming these foods.

14. Can Pregnant women embark on the sirtfood diet?

Once again, try as much as possible to talk to your physician before making any decisions on the sirtfood diet as a pregnant woman. Your baby requires enough nutrition as possible, and restricting calories in this delicate stage may not be such a good idea. You can, however, incorporate the sirtfoods into your diet also. Children also should not embark on a full-scale diet. Instead, they should just be fed a lot of sirtfoods.

15. Must I complete the Seven-day period of Phase One?

For superlative execution, it is recommended that the seven-day period for phase One be completed. However, if for health reasons or any other cogent excuse, you cannot complete the full days, then try to stick to the rules of phase One for a minimum of five days to reap the rewards of the sirtfood diet. If you have a special medical condition such as ulcers, talk to your doctor before embarking on this diet, or simply just incorporate sirtfoods into your regular diet. Note that if you want to repeat the first phase of the diet, you have to wait for a month before going through that seven-day regimen again.

CHAPTER TWELVE
SUMMARY

In this book, we have examined, in great detail, the novel and extremely effective sirtfood diet. In the opening chapter, we promised to go over the mechanism of action of the sirtfood diet, the benefits of the diet, the foods that make up the diet, a shopping list for the foods, recipes for the foods in the sirtfood diet, success stories, a meal plan, and answers to burning questions you might have. We have managed to go through all that and even more. The ball is in your court right now, and it is up to you to put the information that you have garnered from this book into good use. It is not too unusual for people to consume revolutionary information and not put them to good use. A lot of times, it takes just one book or one piece of information to change your life, and to be honest, this book could be your turning point.

The sirtfood diet is so effective because its effects are noticed almost immediately, spurring you on to keep trying to make more progress. As has been described extensively in the book, the foods in the diet are packed with nutrients and biochemicals called polyphenols that would work in tandem with the calorie-restriction policy to help to activate a special set of genes in your body called the sirtuins. The sirtuins would then direct a series of biochemical reactions in your body, which would help to instigate the burning of accumulated fat deposits, enhance fitness and mental alertness, and reduce your susceptibility to chronic diseases in the long term.

The foods that make up the sirtfood diet have also been shown to contain other extremely helpful biochemicals such as antioxidants that help to counteract the effects of free radicals on the body, thereby helping to slow down aging. The anticarcinogenic agents in most of the core sirtfoods help to reduce the risk of cancer. Most of the sirtfoods also contain anti-inflammatory agents that help to prevent inflammations in the long and short term. The sirtfoods are also loaded with a lot of nutrients, which help to boost the immune system, lower blood sugar, correct and manage bone defects and promote the long-term well-being of the human body.

The possibilities that the sirtfood diet offers are practically endless. This is a fortuity for you to make a difference in your life by making a difference to work on what goes into your body. You want to be fit, trim, healthy, and mentally alert? Think about how much more information you could recall and retain, how much you could save in hospital bills, and how much you could achieve with a fitter body. The choice is yours, but I would advise you to get started on this diet right away. Fortune awaits the bold ladies and gentlemen, and finally, I'd like to use this medium to welcome you to a world of uncountable opportunities. Welcome to the Sirtfood Diet!